Accession no.
36220722

KU-743-786

Promoting Resilience

Supporting children and young people who are in care, adopted or in need

Robbie Gilligan

LIS LIBRARY

Date	Fund
04/04/16	xe -Shr

Order No.
2720048

University of Chester

BAAF
ADOPTION
& FOSTERING

Published by
British Association for Adoption & Fostering
(BAAF)
Saffron House
6–10 Kirby Street
London EC1N 8TS
www.baaf.org.uk

Charity registration 275689 (England & Wales)
and SC039337 (Scotland)

© Robbie Gilligan, 2009

British Library Cataloguing in Publication Data
A catalogue record for this book is available from the British Library

ISBN 978 1 905664 13 9

Project management by Shaila Shah
Director of Publications, BAAF

Photographs on covers from iStockphoto.com, posed by models

All photographs posed by models and from iStockphoto.com unless
otherwise indicated

Designed and typeset by Andrew Haig & Associates
Printed in Great Britain by The Lavenham Press
Trade distribution by Turnaround Publisher Services, Unit 3,
Olympia Trading Estate, Coburg Road, London N22 6TZ

All rights reserved. Apart from any fair dealing for the purposes of
research or private study, or criticism or review, as permitted under
the Copyright, Designs and Patents Act 1988, this publication may
not be reproduced, stored in a retrieval system, or transmitted in
any form or by any means, without the prior written permission of
the publishers.

The moral right of the author has been asserted in accordance with
the Copyright, Designs and Patents Act 1988.

BAAF is the leading UK-wide membership organisation for all those
concerned with adoption, fostering and child care issues.

Contents

Acknowledgements

I wish to thank all the foster carers, young people in care, social workers and residential workers whose stories have influenced my thinking and the ideas in this book. I also wish to acknowledge the support of my colleagues in the School of Social Work and Social Policy and the Children's Research Centre, Trinity College, Dublin. Last, but certainly not least, I want to thank my wife, Mary Quinn, and our daughters, Aoife, Sinéad and Orla, for their constant support and for what they have taught me.

Note about the author

Professor Robbie Gilligan is Head of the School of Social Work and Social Policy and Associate Director of The Children's Research Centre at Trinity College Dublin. His publications in the field of child welfare include *Issues in Foster Care* (co-edited with Greg Kelly) and *Promoting Child Development: A guide for child care and protection workers* (co-authored with Brigid Daniel and Sally Wassell), both books published by Jessica Kingsley Publishers, London. He has a special interest in the concept of resilience and its application in work with children in care. He has published papers and presented workshops on this theme in a number of countries.

He has been a youth worker, social worker and foster carer. He has served as a board member of various social service organisations (including the Irish Foster Care Association). He is a member of the Editorial Boards of the journals *Child and Family Social Work, Child Indicators Research* and the *European Journal of Social Work* and of the Advisory Boards of the journals *Children and Society, Adoption & Fostering,* and *Child Care in Practice.*

Foreword

Resilience is one of those hurrah words that everyone is for. Like having a sense of humour, most of us think we have it and think it good that other people should have it too. Approached in this way, resilience sounds as if it is something we have that's innate. It implies strength, both of body and mind, character and attitude. In these senses, the term "resilient" is used as an adjective, a property of the individual that they have in varying degrees. However, the research community is keen to discourage us from thinking about resilience in this fashion. It's too static, too deterministic. It is in danger of missing the point – that resilience is context specific and that we are all more or less resilient depending on the demand being made of us.

Modern psychological definitions of resilience see it as the successful negotiation of a challenge or risk. In other words, you can't show resilience or be resilient until you meet an adverse situation that makes demands of you. If you adapt well to the adverse situation and if you continue to cope well under the pressure, then you are showing resilience. You have functioned well under that stress. Certain characteristics, experiences and attributes may help you cope well with a particular risk, but that same trait may not always confer a benefit when a different kind of risk is met. This approach to resilience sees it as a dynamic "person–environment interaction", a process in which the individual achieves positive adjustment in the face of an adversity (Schoon, 2006, p.17).

Children in residential and foster care generally have more than their fair share of adversity. They meet more risks than most children simply by virtue of being removed from their families of origin, suffering multiple changes of school and friends, and being less well prepared to handle relationships, academic expectations, and life's daily hassles. It is therefore good that carers, social and health workers as well as teachers have taken a real interest in the concept of resilience. The growth of positive psychology and strengths perspectives is part of a welcome shift in the way we think about human development and behaviour. This shift lends itself particularly well to thinking about how best to support children who are in care, adopted or in need.

A key theme running through the promotion of resilience is the value of good relationships. It is within the context of warm, interested, reciprocal relationships that children learn to feel secure, loved, valued, recognised, appreciated, applauded and celebrated. It is where they learn emotional intelligence and social understanding. It is where they develop self-esteem. These skills and understandings help children negotiate risk.

However, there are many other situations that give children the chance to adapt well to risk and enjoy positive experiences. School, sport, art, music, part-time jobs, friends, and relationships with extended birth family members all have the potential to deepen children's understanding, personal resources and sense of worth. They might need support, encouragement and guidance but if they engage and rise to the challenge, they will strengthen their intelligence, skills and understanding so that when they meet new risks, they increase their chances of handling them well.

Reference

Schoon. I. (2006) *Risk and Resilience: Adaptations in changing times*, Cambridge: Cambridge University Press.

Well, that's a sketch of the theory. But how can it be put into practice? In 2001, Robbie Gilligan wrote *Promoting Resilience: A resource guide on working with children in the care system* published by BAAF. It was an instant success. Here was a book that not only explained the concept of resilience but also offered a practical guide about how to promote it in practice. Carers, social workers, health professionals and teachers found the book refreshingly readable and relevant. Rather than tell carers and practitioners what was wrong, it encouraged them to think about how things might be put right. The current edition updates and expands Robbie's earlier book, and a splendid effort it is too, both in terms of content and the high quality of the production, for which Shaila Shah as Director of Publishing and BAAF have to be congratulated.

Packed with examples and ideas, Robbie Gilligan takes the reader on a tour of the wisdom that currently informs resilience and its promotion. Good quality, emotionally attuned relationships remain central. But they can be found and supported not just in the family, but with grandparents, teachers, siblings and friends. A point I particularly liked is Robbie's recognition that children who enjoy opportunities to experience many different social roles are going to increase their chances of finding one that works particularly well for them. Successful social roles also imply positive personal relationships. You can't plan which role or relationship will do the trick, but just giving children the chance to try out new things, meet different people, and experience themselves in fresh ways might open up unexpected possibilities. Nothing beats finding out that you're interested in something, that someone is interested in you being interested, that you begin to feel recognised and good about yourself, so you develop the interest, and so a benign circle sets in.

Promoting Resilience gives the reader hundreds of ideas. You don't have to follow them literally, but what you do get is a feeling of being inspired to think anew and adapt the philosophy to the children with whom you work. Enthusiasm is infectious. Belief spurs you on. And behind all that Robbie writes and says is a celebration of that precious quality of never giving up, of living with hope.

The book is brought alive by many quotes from the children themselves. In the dozens of examples where the children have clearly risen to the occasion, the quotes are uplifting. But to end, here is just one, from 10-year-old Sam, placed for adoption with a gay couple, talking about his two enterprising dads:

> *My dads have made my life so worthwhile because of all the things they do to support me – from helping with the homework to taking me to football. That's what good dads do – even though they are not really interested in football for themselves, they take an interest because it's part of my life. My dads have shown me that I have other abilities too, other than just football. Now I do drama, dance and play the keyboard. I can even cook a three-course meal!*

David Howe
University of East Anglia, Norwich

Why this book?

Helping children in need, in care or who go on to be adopted can be complex and difficult. Or, more correctly, these children's needs are deceptively simple, but delivering the right response to each child is deceptively complex. Whether at the level of a single child in need, or at the level of all children in a regional or national system of out-of-home care, it can be difficult to ensure that the right thing is done all of the time.

The idea to write this book stems from a deep commitment to improving the experience of children in need and those who live in or have lived in the public care system. I hope that social workers and carers will find in it some fresh ideas for how to work with, and on behalf of, children. The main message of the book is one of hope: hope that the lives of these vulnerable children can be made better, even by little things, and hope that what we – social workers and carers - do can make a difference. The book also promotes the message of looking first at strengths and positives in a child's profile and in their social context.

This idea runs counter to a well-embedded tradition in helping and caring services that looks first for the deficits, the pathology, the problem. This book belongs to an exciting tradition that argues the value of seeking out and building on and out from what is positive in the circumstances of a person in need (Saleebey, 1997).

The ideas in the book are drawn from a range of sources. They come from my reading of a range of literature, within psychology, sociology, education and social work relevant to child and social development. They come from courses I have taught in Trinity College, Dublin and from presentations and workshops I have conducted in agencies and universities and at conferences in Australia, Belgium, Britain, Canada, Ethiopia, Hong Kong, Ireland, New Zealand, Sweden, Ukraine and the USA. Feedback from students and participants and the many examples and questions they have raised have stimulated and helped me to develop my ideas. We clearly need more resources to provide good services to vulnerable children – those in the care system, be it in foster families or residential care or those in need. But we also require clear ideas about what it may be helpful to do, why, and when. We can draw on our own experience and the practice wisdom of others, but we owe it to the young people to draw also as much as we can on the best knowledge available in terms of relevant research and thinking from fields such as psychology, sociology, education and social work. If the work is difficult, and if it is worth doing and worth doing well, then we owe it to ourselves and the children to have the best possible knowledge and ideas informing our practice. The stakes are high. What we do affects the children now and in the future, not to mention how it may affect their children and their children's children. We all share a common ambition and moral duty to help children in need or in care to avoid becoming 'another anonymous homeless "statistic" on the streets' (Andreou, 2000, p.78).

I want to acknowledge the help I have received from social workers, foster carers, residential workers, students, and participants at workshops and conferences who have shared questions, ideas, experiences and many telling examples and have helped to reinforce and spark the ideas in this book. The response to the first edition of this book and positive comments about its relevance to work with children in the care system has been sufficiently enthusiastic and positive to prompt me to prepare this second edition with a wider reach. I hope it will help the ideas to reach an even wider audience and stimulate further thinking and ideas for renewing practice. Written out of my Irish experience, the material in the book draws heavily on material garnered abroad as well as from reading, from responses at workshops and from responses to requests for case examples. I have also drawn on a range of research and material published internationally. There is a steady and exciting growth in the range of research evidence relevant to the theme of resilience and its potential application in fields of professional practice. This makes the task of preparing the second edition both challenging and rewarding.

In acknowledging the many influences on my thinking, I also wish to salute the resilience of young people who do well and the efforts of the social workers and carers and adoptive parents who foster that resilience despite the many stresses of their roles.

The book is written in a way that seeks to give a direct voice to the experience of young people. The reader will find extracts drawn from research on their lives as well as quotes from young people themselves. In addition, there are many quotes from other sources which illuminate the realities and possibilities of living in care. In many sections, the reader is offered questions or exercises that can be used to stimulate private reflection or group discussion.

1 Life in care

You're not comfortable in one place; you're bound to move. You don't know what to call home. I never stay in one place. I moved four times in the past years. It does affect you. You don't know what to call home. Especially when you get into a relationship. It is hard to stay in one place. I moved from the time I was two, even before foster care. It has been unstable. I moved so much. I can't stay in one place.

(Young person in care who had seven moves with no returns home, quoted in Unrau et al, 2008)

Being in care

> They [foster youth] go through a constant state of loss. They lose their families first. Then they often lose one foster family after another for lots of times, things that have nothing to do with them. And they lose their friends. They lose their school. They lose their neighbourhood, their sense of who they are and where they belong. And it's just a series of losses until finally, I think a lot of kids just feel empty.
>
> *(Social worker quoted in Geenan and Powers, 2007, p. 1093)*

For some young people, life in the care system can offer a fresh start, and with it the opportunity to make something of their lives. For many others, the outcomes may not be so positive as the challenging quote above hints. The problems that brought them into care may not have been resolved; indeed, in some cases these problems may have got worse. Accordingly, life in care may not equip them well to cope with life afterwards.

Being in local authority care may mean young people are cut off from supports that may have worked well for them in their previous life. Living in care may thus mean they end up short of people who are concerned for them and committed to them over the long haul. Living in care may also mean disruption and problems in the young person's education. Such educational difficulties risk blocking one of the possible escape routes for youngsters from the disadvantages of care and the factors that led to their being in care. For young people in care the worst aspect of the experience may be the sense that at the end of the day nobody really *cares* about *you*. There may also be the lesson for some that you can't really rely on what adults say to you.

Children from minority ethnic communities may also have their cultural background and extended family resources neglected. Decisions by social workers and carers may be insensitive to the strengths and assets of the traditions and networks to which minority ethnic children belong. The following extract from a report on a statutory inspection of services in England illustrates this point.

> One family told us of workers' reluctance to place children with grandparents because their accommodation was inadequate. The children were placed with foster carers whose accommodation in the family's eyes was also inadequate – both properties had the same number of bedrooms. The placement was also not sympathetic to the children's religious needs and there was resistance to their wearing of traditional dress. Another family believed the potential of relatives to offer care to a young person was not given enough consideration, resulting in a placement away from home.
>
> *(O'Neale, 2000, p.22)*

But similar issues may also apply for the general body of children in care.

> I'm going to leave here soon and who have I got? Nobody. Don't get me wrong, they have done a lot for me here and I'll carry on coming in 'cos I'll only be living down the road in a flat. I'll probably drop in most nights, in fact. But I've got no friends of my own. God knows how many schools I've been to and I'm not the easiest person to make friends with. I haven't seen my Mum now for six years – I don't even know where she lives. They stopped me from seeing her when I was younger. Who have I got left, eh? Tell me!

> *(Young person in residential care quoted in Berridge, 1985, p.108)*

Trevor, in care for 16 years

Trevor's future is bleak. He has no family and no friends of his own age outside his children's home. He may maintain some contact with his last foster family and keep in touch with the children's home but apart from this he will be totally isolated. Thus his situation will be highly precarious. Although he has been in care for 16 years, he will emerge with little emotional, educational, social and economic capital.

(Berridge, 1985, p.50)

For many young people in care, their experiences may make it difficult to trust adults, and this may become an issue right through their adult life.

> It made it real difficult to trust people . . . I have become more guarded 'cause I get so scared to lose somebody. It takes me a long time to drop my guard . . . As soon as they are nice to me, I automatically think they want something. I become really defensive. It made it difficult for me to become attached . . . Eventually I became an angry, angry person who could not trust anybody.

> *(Young person who had eight moves while in care with no returns home, quoted in Unrau et al, 2008.)*

> You're not comfortable in one place; you're bound to move. You don't know what to call home. I never stay in one place. I moved four times in the past years. It does affect you. You don't know what to call home. Especially when you get into a relationship. It is hard to stay in one place. I moved from the

time I was two, even before foster care. It has been unstable. I moved so much. I can't stay in one place.

(Young person in care who had seven moves with no returns home, quoted in Unrau et al, 2008.)

The issues facing children in care are not just about where they will live or get support. There are other uncertainties and disadvantages that may face them.

Sometimes I get really scared 'cause sometimes I get worried that I have to move again and I don't want to move ever again. 'Cause I don't want to lose all my friends as well.

(Eight-year-old girl, quoted in Fernandez, 2007)

I never had a desk where I could work or anything like that. There wasn't like a room where you could sort of go and you knew fine, well, it would be quiet to be able to study.

('Natasha Gates' quoted in Martin and Jackson, 2002, p. 126)

I've had to move school quite a lot, make new friends and that. All the schools do the work in a different way so that's been hard, having to catch up all the time.

(Claire quoted in Happer et al, 2006, p. 21)

You really feel like you're just a file, you know? It's like they do have a lot of kids to take care of and there's other people with worse situations, that's why I understand, I get it. But, you want more than that, you know?

(Greeson and Bowen, 2008, p. 1185)

While the following experience may seem extreme and hopefully things have improved somewhat, it is undoubtedly the case that many young people in care today may still identify with some of what this boy is saying:

I had three foster home placements in two years after I was taken into care and I then ended up in a children's home. I hadn't much of a clue as to where I came from and none about where I was going. Nobody seemed to care about me, they never asked me what I wanted or what I felt, never showed interest in what I did, either in school, in sport or in anything. Unless, of course, you nicked something or kicked up rough, then there was hell to pay and everyone put their nose in.

(Boy quoted in Bullock et al, 1993, p.126)

2 The concept of resilience

Resilience is about doing well in the face of adversity. Resilience comprises a set of qualities that may help a person to withstand many of the negative effects of adversity. A child displaying resilience has more positive outcomes than might be expected given the level of adversity impinging on their development.

Defining resilience

Resilience is about doing well in the face of adversity. Resilience comprises a set of qualities that may help a person to withstand many of the negative effects of adversity. A child displaying resilience has more positive outcomes than might be expected given the level of adversity impinging on their development. Bearing in mind what has happened to them, a resilient child does better than he or she ought to do. Understanding why some children may make favourable progress in unfavourable circumstances may tell us more about how to help people exposed to potentially damaging experiences. It may be useful to consider three dimensions of resilience:

- **overcoming the odds** – being successful despite exposure to high risk;

- **sustaining competence under pressure** - adapting to high risk;

- **recovering from trauma** - adjusting successfully to negative life events.

(Fraser et al, *1999, p.136)*

Using this framework, we may see how a young person in care may demonstrate these various aspects of resilience. They may continue to do well socially and academically despite having endured abusive or adverse experiences at home prior to coming into local authority care. Despite the pressure of being separated from family and the related tensions, a young person may still prove able to do reasonably well at school and successfully hold down a part-time job. The youngster in care showing resilience may be able to recover from the trauma of neglect and court-ordered removal to care, the ensuing separation, and the ambivalent and fraught relations with parents.

A resilient youngster is one who adapts positively in the face of risky circumstances. They do better than might reasonably be expected.

What accounts for why some youngsters may be resilient in the face of risk and adversity, at least some of the time? It is a complicated picture and one which research is still trying to clarify. The answer seems to lie in the complex interaction between:

- the nature of the risk and adversity involved;

- the qualities and experiences of the young person; and

- the qualities of the relationships and environment in which the young person is growing up.

While individual attributes may be important, it should be remembered that resilience emerges in a supportive *context* (Fraser *et al*, 1999). Different props and supports may promote and sustain resilience in different sets of circumstances. Depending on the context, these props and supports may often be quite simple. For example, in the case of a person in middle age, a pair of spectacles may be a magical source of resilience in the face of the adversity of failing sight. Spectacles are the simple prop which allow the person to release once again their natural urge and capacity for reading. In our work with young people, the key may often be finding an equivalent prop or props, which may help to sustain them day to day. As with the spectacles, it may often be something simple that makes the big difference.

The following are some key propositions that may help illuminate the concept of resilience.

© Digital Vision

- It may be helpful to think of people's development as progressing along a pathway. What happens next is influenced, but not determined, by what goes before.

- People are not passive bystanders in the process of their own development. From the youngest age, children have a degree of *agency* or influence in terms of what happens next in their developmental progress. But events in their lives – big and small – and the social context in which these occur are also very influential in shaping progress along the developmental path and how the growing person interacts with and responds to these experiences. A foster mother who likes to read to her foster child may help to sow the seed of a life-time's love of reading, an achievement that is significant not just for the immediate enjoyment it offers, but also for the key part that reading skills play in educational progress, and also for the warm memory and positive modelling of caring that the simple act of reading aloud to a young person may lay down.

- Adverse experiences of sufficient severity may block the child's natural drive for development and healing. Resilience, where it operates, may serve to release again the natural flow of recovery and development that might otherwise be paralysed or frozen by negative experiences.

- It seems that children who display resilience do not possess 'mysterious or unique qualities', but instead have access to supportive and protective resources in their lives to help buffer them against the effects of adverse environments and circumstances (Masten and Coatsworth, 1998).

- People acquire whatever qualities of resilience they may possess in two ways – by what they are born with through their genes, and by the effects of subsequent social experience. Positive home experiences, positive school experiences, positive experiences in leisure-time interests and so on may singly or, in some combination, play a part in enhancing resilience.

- As carers, social workers or educators, we are able to influence only that portion of resilience that is amenable to influence through social experience. We cannot affect the degree of resilience that a person has temperamentally due to what they have inherited through their genes, although it now seems that how genetic influence plays out may be affected by life experience.

- Resilience should not be regarded as some new modern code word for moral fibre or moral character. We must not end up blaming a victim of unfavourable social circumstances for being the author of their own downfall because they lack social resilience. A social resilience perspective most definitely does *not* seek to shift the burden of rescue/recovery/rehabilitation/change onto the victim of adversity.

- It is essential to remember that it is the social context in which the person lives their life that influences whether and how resilience is displayed. It is this social context that fosters or inhibits the latent or manifest qualities of resilience that the young person may or may not display.

- Services can enhance resilience in young people in care or in need by positively influencing social experiences and social resources available to them, their carers and their family of origin.

- Formal services and professional interventions must avoid aggravating or prolonging problems unnecessarily by failing to see the potential for resilience in a young person or their social context.

- Someone may show resilience in certain contexts, but not in every part of their life. There may be a mixed picture. Despite living in care and coping with the trauma of family break up, a young person may still be a successful athlete, even if not exactly a star, academically, at school. A young woman in care following serious sexual abuse may be a high achieving student, but may also be lacking in confidence in her relations with peers. School, as a separate "domain", may serve as a kind of asylum for such young people. The young person may be faring quite differently in different domains, displaying resilience in some but not others.

- A key message for practice is helping the person to hang on to and build on positive factors, threads and niches in their lives. It may also be about tapping into the commitment of strong positive elements in the child's social network. It may, for example, be about helping them to connect to a strong and interested grandparent who is willing to support the child in different ways.

- A social resilience perspective encourages the harnessing of the energy of the child, family, informal helpers and services. It helps to target promising pressure points for change in a child's social ecology.

- We should not forget that protective factors that enhance resilience might not always be positive experiences. Sometimes surviving hardship of some kind may make a person stronger and more resilient.

- Since resources are always scarcer than need, it is relevant that a social resilience perspective may help to unearth and release some fresh and unrecognised resources in a child's daily life and natural social networks.

- Serendipity may sometimes, unexpectedly, play a good hand to a young person in difficult circumstances.

- Young people may unexpectedly befriend an interested adult who is willing to play an ongoing role in the child's life. It is important for professionals and formal services not to get in the way of making the most of this favourable hand.

- A child who may show resilience is not invulnerable. Children cannot withstand unscathed, ever-increasing levels of stress. Past a certain threshold of increasing adversity, any child is likely to buckle and succumb to the pressure.

- Reducing the number of negative factors in a child's life may thus be helpful as a way of giving the potential effect of positive factors a better chance of kicking in. Even where it is not possible to reduce negative factors, adding one or more positive factors may lead to a more favourable balance in the child's life. It may be helpful to think of the image of a set of weighing scales with negative or adverse weights on one side, and positive or protective weights on the other. The aim is to tilt the balance in the child's life in favour of protective factors. Using the image of the weighing scales, this more favourable balance can be achieved either by removing a sufficient number of weights from the negative side, or by adding sufficient countervailing weights to the positive side. It may sometimes be more possible to add positive weights than remove negative weights. For example, it may be very difficult to erase in the short term the impact of a father's alcoholism and domestic violence. It may be easier to add the value of the positive support of an aunt and an interested teacher. Even if it is not possible to tilt the balance in the favourable direction, the message from research seems to be to reduce the total number of negative weights, or at least their net effect, when the value of positive weights are counted in.

- A resilience-led perspective fits well with the current emphasis on *outcomes* in social service design and evaluation. A resilience-led perspective highlights the importance of building the long-run capacity of the young person and supportiveness of the social contexts in which they live out their lives.

- While a strengths or resilience-led perspective may have much to offer, it is unrealistic and unhelpful to rely exclusively on such a perspective, especially in circumstances of extreme adversity (Fraser *et al*, 1999).

Practice implications of a resilience-led perspective

A resilience-led perspective tends to be optimistic and pragmatic. It believes that change is often possible, even in unpromising conditions, and that change may start in simple ways: one thinks the glass is half full rather than half empty. The following propositions seem to sum up the meaning of the overall approach.

- Change is possible.

- Change may come through *supportive relationships*.

- Change may also come through new ways of thinking about problems and possibilities.

- Change can sometimes come from little things, for example, from seemingly mundane daily experience.

- Change may begin in one small part of a person's life.

- Change can grow from the ordinary and the everyday; it does not have to come from specialist or clinical sources.

- Change may come from a single opportunity or positive turning point which leads on to other good things.

- Change may come from tapping into strengths in a child's circumstances, strengths that may have long gone unrecognised.

- Change may sometimes come through chance - chance experiences, chance contacts which, if allowed, may lead on to positive outcomes.

- Getting some things right, even one thing, may be the best place to start.

- It is more helpful to look first for strengths and possibilities.

- Daily life is often filled with many natural and helpful opportunities.

- The people who are likely to be around longest for a child are relatives and other people in their informal social networks. Siblings may be particularly important because they share so much in common with the young person. Siblings, alone, may understand best the child's story and experience.

- The child can be one of the agents of change and development in their own lives.

- Help should aim to add to, rather than cut off, good things that are already in a child's life.

- Complex problems rarely have single answers - often progress lies in attention to a whole series of smaller steps which may interact with each other in positive and sometimes unforeseen ways.

- "The best may be the enemy of the good" - waiting to achieve the elusive best possible solution may mean that, in the meanwhile, the potential good of valuable intermediate steps may be overlooked or missed and the overall problem is thus, unnecessarily, made more intractable.

- Big plans have a habit of coming unstuck (Cooper and Webb, 1999). It may be best not to have "all the eggs in one basket" in terms of planning.

- "One size fits all" solutions are unlikely to work. Positive change is more likely to flow from approaches that are tailored to the circumstances and experiences of each individual child.

Positive "turning" points in developmental pathways – a key idea in resilience thinking

It is possible to map the development of a child as if along a pathway with its different twists and turns. For some children, the pathway follows its expected course and, barring something very unforeseen, what is to come can more or less be predicted from what has gone before. At the risk of over-simplifying, good things tend to lead to more good things, bad things to more bad things. But the die is certainly not cast. For some children, something - good or bad - may happen in the form of a turning point experience. A positive turning point may help to turn a child's life around. Recognising such possible turning points becomes important as the vignette overleaf illustrates.

The stories of Patrick and Rose

Consider the following scenarios for Patrick and Rose. The accumulation of favourable life experiences sets Patrick off on a positive pathway. His mother is healthy, has a stress-free pregnancy and a straightforward birth; home is comfortable and not short of money, the father is supportive and there are good relations with extended family and neighbours. Over time, family health remains good and transition to school, social relations with peers and educational attainments are accomplished relatively easily.

On the other hand, the accumulation of negative factors and processes sets Rose off on a negative and risky pathway. Her mother has poverty-related physical and mental health problems and a conflictual relationship with Rose's father. Coming home from hospital with the new baby, Rose's mother is faced with limited money and limited support. Entry to school also proves a stressful transition for Rose, who lacks easy skills and confidence in relating to her peers.

What happens next for Patrick and Rose depends on what has gone before and on events or incidents that may change the picture. Patrick will continue to do well, unless circumstances change dramatically as in the following scenario. His parents decide to move abroad when he is six years old to a much better paying job for the father. Some time later, the parents' marriage breaks up and the mother, who gains custody, feels isolated and depressed and is slow to seek family help. Patrick's social confidence and school performance are badly affected by developments at home.

A slightly different picture develops in the case of Rose. Her mother sets up home on her own and gets on well with supportive neighbours who help her with child care so that she can take up a morale- and income-enhancing job. Some years later she meets a new partner and he eventually moves in. He has a very positive relationship with Rose and encourages her in her talent for hockey. The combined effect of more money, more contentment and more support at home means that things are looking a great deal brighter for Rose as her development unfolds.

Quite often it is relatively small things which can make a difference. The good luck of finding (or probably more correctly the capacity to connect with) supportive neighbours helped begin to turn things around for Rose and her mother. Moving abroad seemed to set off an unexpected series of negative events for Patrick.

Turning points are significant as we seek to understand the dynamics of a child's development. They may prove to have positive or negative effects.

Patrick and Rose's stories contain good examples of such positive and negative turning points – Patrick was badly affected by his parents' marriage breakdown. Rose was positively affected by the benign impact of a new partner in her mother's life.

Declan's story below illustrates again the power of a positive turning point, this time represented by foster carers who pushed that little bit harder and showed Declan that they had high expectations of him.

Declan: expectations that paid off

Before we started fostering, Sian and I had run homes in the community for adults with learning disabilities. So we don't believe in limits, we push children that little bit harder to see what they can do. We showed Declan that there are no boundaries. We had higher expectations for him than for other children and he met them. If you plant the idea then a child turns it over in their head and begins to think of themselves as someone who can achieve.

Declan achieved all sorts of things while he was with us. He got a Royal Yachting Association Qualification and was competent to take a small dinghy out on his own. We'd introduced him to the Sea Cadets but his sense of danger was so lacking that they said they couldn't have him because he'd been about to walk off the harbour wall and fall 20 feet into the sea. But we're very fortunate as there's a set of schemes for local young people and Declan went on a taster day. The sailing came out of this. The scheme immediately put in one-to-one support for him, and as he learnt to do more and more things for himself, the one-to-one support was withdrawn. Declan was doing very well in education and the school put a lot of effort into helping him. Despite his moderate learning disabilities, he studied for four GCSEs, which he'd probably have passed. When he came to us he could not write his name; 12 months later he was reading the Goosebumps book series. We have an expectation that all our children will attend school and do their best, and with Declan that paid off.

(Foster carer quoted in Bond (ed), 2005, pp. 118-19)

Turning points in a young person's unfolding life involve two key elements. These are:

- **opportunities** presented to the person in the form of, for example, a job or in the form of a relationship (for example, a marriage to a stable, committed partner); and

- **capacity**, an openness, and most crucially a willingness on the part of the person, at that moment of presentation of the opening to engage with the opportunity. A person's sense of agency plays a crucial part in seizing the moment, in actually harvesting the benefit that can flow from a potentially positive turning point.

> A major turning point has the potential to open a system the way a key has the potential to open a lock ... action is necessary to complete the turning.

(Abbott, 1997, pp. 96-97, quoted in Laub and Sampson, 2003, p. 282)

While the action to take up a positive opportunity must largely be the person's own, it seems reasonable to claim that well attuned supportive activity by caring adults or others may also be relevant.

Returning to the examples of the job or the marriage above, the person's agency is evident not only in the choice to enter into the job or the marriage, but also in the commitment to keep their part of the bargain going.

Serendipity and turning points

Chance may play a big part in offering a potential turning point opportunity, but the young person must take the opportunity to gain the benefit, as this story illustrates.

A hidden talent

A teenage boy lived in a residential unit. In his eyes, not much happened there and he spent his time being bored and disaffected. One day he began to rummage in some cupboards whose contents had long been forgotten. In one he found an old electronic keyboard. He took it out and began to try to play it. Gradually he discovered a hidden talent. From scratch, and without any tuition (but probably with a lot of patience from staff and fellow residents), he slowly mastered the techniques required. He now earns a living as a professional musician in one of the major holiday resorts.

(Example from conference participant)

Things to note

Before concluding this discussion on turning points, there are three important things to note:

- Turning point experiences may not always prove positive in their effect, they may sometimes be negative - take, for example, the case of a road accident which may give rise to injuries with longer-term adverse consequences.

- Turning points may only emerge as significant in retrospect; at the time their longer-term importance may not have been very obvious - take, for example, a brief friendship that led to being informed about a job vacancy which the person

© Digital Vision

pursued and which led to them thriving in the world of work for the first time in their life, and continuing to do so long after the friendship has ended.

- Turning points play a relatively small part in the emergence of resilience. They may not be a factor in every life where resilience may be displayed at some point. While turning points with positive impact should certainly be recognised and valued, it is really the case that nature and nurture are probably more important. In terms of interventions, the issue is really about influencing nurture, which, for all practical purposes in the case of children in care, is above all about helping children find and hold onto (positive) 'strong relationships with adults' (Luthar *et al*, 2006). Another way of putting this is to say that favourable "turning point moments" may help, but what really sustains resilience for young people is long-term commitment in the form of strong supportive relationships with adults.

So what influences whether young people can have 'strong relationships with adults'? The availability of adults in relevant roles – parents, carers, older siblings, other relatives, professionals, teachers, mentors and so on is clearly critical. The capacity of the young person to engage in, and sustain, a relationship with an adult is also important. Self-esteem, social skills and other factors may play a part in this. Gender may be important – there is some evidence that girls may be better at key social skills such as chatting to people and this may help them to be better than boys at building and sustaining supportive contact and relationships.

Below is an example of the key role that a mental health specialist was able to play in the life of a young unaccompanied asylum-seeking woman, Rakeb, who had suffered memory loss as a result of the various traumas she had experienced.

> For me, my psychologist was like part of my family because, first, I was growing up in her hands and second, she put everything back inside me which I losted [sic]. I lost my personality, I lost my memory, I lost my confidence for a while and she put everything back inside. She took me back to my personality, to my qualities inside me . . . All of me is back.
>
> *(Rakeb, quoted in Chase et al, 2008, p. 57)*

Sometimes, peers can also play a vital role, as in the example below.

> Meeting other transracially adopted people . . . For years, I wondered if it was true that nobody but me feels like this. Am I being ungrateful and should I feel very lucky because who wants to grow up in an orphanage? Then, when I met another transracially adopted person who said, 'I feel like that too,' my feelings were validated. Meeting another transracially adopted person was really, really good – very cathartic in some ways. I was able to express how I felt without having to justify my feelings and without anyone being hurt or offended. We were able to share experiences safely.
>
> *(Chris Atkins, quoted in Harris (ed), 2006, pp. 284-5)*

3 Key social ingredients of resilience:
Social roles, secure base, identity, self-esteem and self-efficacy

I found these lovely people . . . you know, it is just like a god-given family. I can't say they replaced my family but they were like there for me so much they become a family to me now. And you know they took care of me . . . she prepared a bath for me, everything, gave me new clothes . . . really lovely people. And they cooked for me and they said you can eat as much as you want . . . They made me feel so comfortable – they made me feel at home.

(Nadine, quoted in Chase et al, 2008, p. 67)

The importance of multiple social roles for the young person in care

Just as actors play roles on stage or in film, or lawyers play roles in the court room, the disciplines of sociology and social psychology remind us that in ordinary everyday living people also play out different **social roles**. One person may possibly play the roles of parent, spouse, brother, son, neighbour and worker. Another may play those of mother, sister, daughter, neighbour, and member of the parents' committee in her child's school. Just as the actor and the lawyer move from one role to another with each new context or assignment, so do ordinary people – old and young – move from one role to another in everyday life. Each person may thus be said to have a number of roles as they live out their lives. These roles may be said to make up a *role set* in which each role entails a slightly different identity. In other words, people wear a number of different "hats" in their daily life.

Research evidence suggests that it is protective of mental health to have such a set of multiple role identities (Thoits, 1983). Too restricted a set of role identities may put the person at risk psychologically. It may be very unhelpful for a person to be virtually trapped in one master role identity, for instance, that of young and poor lone parent. Similarly, it is likely to be unhelpful for a young person to have as his or her exclusive or *master identity* that of being, or having been, " in care". This is not to deny the significance of being in care. Rather it is to stress that being in care is not the whole story about the young person. Being in care should not dominate the young person's sense of self as seen by themselves and others, to the extent that it erases other facets of the young person's identity and "story".

What is the relevance of this point when working with young people in care? For the young person in care, it suggests that he or she may benefit from taking on further role identities beyond what is unfortunately, sometimes, the devalued or stigmatised master identity of "young person in care". What such role identities might realistically be available to him or her? The different arenas in which we live our lives – home, extended family, neighbourhood, school, workplace, friendship networks, clubs, faith community – provide a range of opportunities for extending our role set, or the range of social roles which we can play. The young person in care might thus be a school student, a sports club member, a singer in the school choir, a regular worshipper or volunteer in their faith community, and a part-time worker in a local fast food outlet.

These multiple role identities can play an important part in protecting the young person's mental health. They can also help release the young person from being trapped in what otherwise might be the isolated ghetto of life in the care system. This set of role identities may also play a part in enhancing the young person's social network in the immediate and longer term. At a very simple level, having a number of roles or role identities means that the young person does not have "all their eggs in one basket", in terms of social support or social development. If relationships go sour in one arena or in one set of connections, it does not mean that *all* of the young person's social relations are thereby in jeopardy.

Besides the value of having a reasonable number of social roles in one's life, there is also the question of how the person views those roles. It is likely that the person will benefit if they have one or more social roles that they consider meaningful (Bifulco and Moran, 1998). For example, the young person may benefit from playing the social role of production team member in the school musical, or from volunteering in a local environmental improvement scheme, or substituting on a school volleyball team. The benefits of each such role include the positive meaning they hold for the young person, linked no doubt also to the social recognition and enjoyment that he or she derives from them. It is important to stress that the benefits are not necessarily linked to the social visibility or prestige of the role. Clearly it does not hurt if what the young person is doing is well regarded, but ultimately it is the value which the young person places on it which seems to matter most.

POINTS TO CONSIDER

Multiple social roles

In the case of a young person in care known to you, list all the social roles he/she plays and consider which roles, if any, are meaningful in a positive sense.

Think of which of the social roles that he/she has acquired through experience (rather than inherited through birth) is now most important for the young person.

Think of how the young person came to take on and play this social role. What people or conditions helped this to happen?

Think of ways in which carers might sensitively encourage young people in their care to try out even one possible new social role.

Think of a young person in care you know – and for whom things are not going all that smoothly right now – and identify the arenas in which he/she plays out their daily life, and consider whether any of these arenas might serve as an "arena of comfort", especially when compared to how things are going in other arenas.

What options might there be to offer young people appropriate work experience, using contacts from:

a) their social networks,

b) their families,

c) the networks of carers, or

d) formal schemes?

What would be a helpful way to "sell" the needs of the young person in care in a positive way to someone who might offer the young person work experience?

In addition, returning to the linked idea of different arenas within which we live our lives, it seems that young people experiencing adversity (such as life in care) may do better if they manage to find an 'arena of comfort' in their lives (Thiede Call, 1996). This is an arena in which things go reasonably well, even if it seems things are going badly or almost falling apart in others. Thus, a young woman who is finding it hard going at home and in school, may cope better if she manages to land a part-time job in the local "chippy", where the owner grows to like her and sees quite different sides to her personality, compared to those which the foster carer or school teachers dislike. This comparative success in the world of work and the support of the "chippy" owner may mean that this part-time job proves to be an important anchor for the young person as she tries to negotiate the otherwise choppy seas of a difficult time in her life.

A transformational experience

A young lone parent struggled in her adjustment to being a parent to her pre-school child. But she was very successful at sport in a community that prized sporting achievement. Success in the domain of sport began to spill into other domains in her life. Members of her immediate and extended family began to offer a lot of help with the care of her child. And she began to see how better skills at reading and better education generally could help her career and progress as a sportswoman. Education had previously been an area of failure in her life. Her involvement in sport was now transforming her attitude towards the value of learning.

(Example from workshop participant)

The importance of a sense of secure base – stable care and continuous relationships

The concept of a **secure base** (drawing on John Bowlby's attachment theory (1988)) relates to the physical and emotional ties that support and sustain us in our growth and development and which console us in times of distress. The secure base is where we move on from when we feel safe and to where we return in times of crisis, confident that we will get the help and support we need. For the small toddler, the secure base is the familiar space and people that constitute his or her immediate and constant social world. The constancy of these people convinces the child that people and the world are fundamentally safe and reliable and that exploring it is a safe, rewarding and enjoyable thing to do. As we grow older, the relationships and places that constitute our secure base may expand but fundamentally we never lose that need for support, encouragement and consolation, nor for the certainty that they will be forthcoming when we need them.

There's never been a photo of me and I never had a birthday party. I'd like to have all the things I missed out on as a child. I'd like to have a birthday party, and just once I'd like to have a birthday cake and blow out all the candles.

(Young Australian formerly in care reflecting on the implications of having been in care, quoted in Cashmore and Paxman, 1996, p.155)

For children in the care system the story is not so simple; it is not always so obvious to them that they have a secure base in the world, a guaranteed set of people who have an unshakeable and partisan commitment to their well-being. Leaving home and living in care may mean fragile relationships are broken, some never to recover. At the age when they are old enough to leave care, at least some care-leavers may be faced with the dilemma of not having an emotional "base camp", that is, a set of people who will dedicate themselves as necessary to supporting and resourcing the young person's journey of exploration and discovery in the world. Enduring relationships with committed people become very important for young people growing up in care. It is from these relationships that their "secure base" may emerge, as Nadine, an unaccompanied asylum-seeking 15-year-old from Rwanda, describes.

I found these lovely people . . . you know, it is just like a god-given family. I can't say they replaced my family but they were like there for me so much they become a family to me now. And you know they took care of me . . . she prepared a bath for me, everything, gave me new clothes . . . really lovely people. And they cooked for me and they said you can eat as much as you want . . . They made me feel so comfortable – they made me feel at home.

(Nadine, quoted in Chase et al, 2008, p. 67)

And 10-year-old Sam, placed for adoption with a gay couple, has this to say:

My dads have made my life so worthwhile because of all the things they do to support me – from helping with homework to taking me to football. That's what good dads do – even though they are not really interested in football for themselves, they take a keen interest because it's a part of my life. My dads have shown me that I have other abilities too, other than just football. Now I do drama, dance and play the keyboard. I can even cook a three-course meal!

© Digital Vision

21

They always have high expectations of me and want me to do well in my life. They've shown me how to dig deep into myself and reach for the best parts. Parts sometimes buried deeply under a lot of sadness. They've taught me how to aim high and achieve my goals.

(Sam, quoted in Bond (ed), 2005, p. 43)

Stability and continuity

Jackson and Thomas (1999) make an important distinction between *stability* and *continuity* in assessing the quality of placement and care experience. They use *stability* in the sense of the child remaining in the same placement, that is, with the same people or in the same place. The young person gets a chance to put down some roots. The deeper these roots go down, the better chance the young person may have to be resilient in the face of adversity. If one thinks of trees in a storm, their chances of withstanding very severe gusts and not being blown down are linked to how deep and secure their roots are. Similarly, the young person in care may be more likely to be able to withstand the "gusts of adversity" in their life if their roots go deep.

POINTS TO CONSIDER

Please think about the conditions that may have caused the death of the tree (on the left). In a sense that tree might be said to have had an unsuccessful placement in that soil, in that place at that time. What might we learn from the reaction of trees that might be relevant to the placement of children?

Continuity refers to the absence of serious disruption to 'the child's networks of relationships, their personal and cultural identity, and their education and health care' (Jackson and Thomas, 1999, p.19). To use the tree metaphor again, if one transplants a tree or plant, it is usually seen as a very delicate process whose success depends on timing and other factors. A key factor may be keeping the roots in familiar soil, so the tree may change place but not soil. For the young person, remaining in familiar "emotional soil" in terms of the continuing ties to family, network and culture may be very important to sustain growth and development in the new placement. Even where there have been serious difficulties, positive relations with parents may prove possible at different points along the way and may bring great consolation for the child or young person:

> (About a biological father) I've never doubted that he really wanted and loved us, though he wasn't the kind of man to ever have said so out loud.
>
> *(Mike, a boy in care, quoted in Happer et al, 2006, p. 23)*

> (About a biological father) . . . I'd like to see him a lot more, heaps and heaps and heaps more times, it makes me feel happy.
>
> *(Eight-year-old girl in care, quoted in Fernandez, 2007, p.352)*

> (About a biological mother) I ask her a lot of questions, I ask her what was she like when she was little . . . Just to see her. That I have an opportunity to talk to her and I think she's glad that she sees me 'cause she has an opportunity to apologise for what she done.
>
> *(17-year-old young woman in care, quoted in Fernandez, 2007, p. 352)*

Relationships in the new placement do not have to *replace* what went before; instead they should *add* to what is good and nurturing from the past. The new placement might be thought of as "fertiliser" to promote growth and health in the faltering and fragile plant and its surrounding soil. Links to the past do not connect only with what is recalled as good. It is also important not to erase or deny relationships which are painful or emotionally ambiguous. It does not follow that a relationship that today looks broken and beyond repair will never again come to have positive meaning and value. Troubled relations may come good with the passage of time and the mellowing of feelings. Even where such reconciliation does not actually occur, the relationships are still likely to have meaning and to have an effect on forward progress for the young person.

Resolving or coming to terms with hurt in past relationships requires revisiting those relationships at least in a metaphorical or symbolic, if not a physical, sense. Moving on from these relationships requires some kind of connection with them. Reconciliation with the past or with people cannot happen if that past or those people cannot be recalled – to memory or to living contact – if and when the young person is ready and feels the need. The planning and pacing of such revisiting of contentious or dormant relationships have to be very carefully considered, in the light of the child's stage of development and the evolution of the child's placement. Such reconnecting to past relationships has to be sensitively matched to the wishes and capacity of the young person. Adults must avoid responding to their own anxiety or impatience, rather than to the child's true need.

Possible outcomes of different combinations of stability and continuity

Both stability and continuity are important for a child's development and well-being. It is possible, as Jackson and Thomas (1999) point out, to have one without the other: a child may have stability and lack continuity. He or she may live in the one place but miss out on continuity in key relationships and experiences, which entering the care system has severed or interrupted. Fortunately for many children, it may be possible for them to experience stability *and* continuity. But this does not just happen automatically. It requires awareness, sensitivity and effort on the part of carers, social workers and key members of the child's social network. It also requires consistency where changes in personnel occur. A new social worker or unit head of a children's home may have a different view about how much to prioritise the preservation of ties to the past. A child may become confused and disillusioned if one day they are encouraged and facilitated in keeping ties alive, and the next day they are discouraged and impeded, all because of the different personal assumptions of newcomer adults, compared to those of adults who have just left. It is also important to remember that at different stages of development the young person may view relationships with certain people differently. People discounted when younger may seem more important when older. It is a service to a young person growing up to keep the possibility of contact alive by helping them keep track of phone numbers and addresses and unfolding changes in the lives of people important to them.

At different stages of development, different sets of relationships may offer a precious sense of commitment and stability. These relationships may not always involve family members or carers, as part of the following story of Matthew, a severely disfigured boy in foster care, testifies.

© Digital Vision

Matthew, a sense of belonging

Matthew went through school rather than to school. He went as regularly as his operations allowed. He had a lot of fun and made a lot of friends but academically he came out with nothing. He still has trouble reading and writing and doesn't always understand forms. Soon after Matthew came to us we moved to a new area, to a larger house, and he changed to a Catholic school because the one nearer us said they had no vacancies. Matthew became very religious for quite a long period and it suited him. He needed that kind of commitment. He sang in the choir and he was an altar boy. For a time he wanted to become a priest. He grew out of it but it helped him although we don't know how. It might have been the friendship or it might have been the beliefs. Now he doesn't attend church but he's kept in touch with the friends he made there.

(Chris, foster mother of Matthew, quoted in Argent, 1998, p.210)

Matthew's story underlines the positive value of experiencing belonging within the community and within friendship groups. As is so often the case, these opportunities grow organically from everyday experience. For Matthew, they grew through a school connection which notably was itself due to a chance (and, as it happens, negative) incident.

How might the stability of placements be enhanced? McAuley and Trew (2000) report findings from a prospective study of 19 foster children aged four to 11 and suggest that foster carers' early assessment of children's behaviour may be a good predictor of later placement-threatening difficulties. The systematic gathering of foster carers' perceptions early in placement may thus help to identify instances where extra support and advice to the carer may be indicated, such as support and advice which might help a placement to survive and continue on a positive note.

Key concepts

Five key concepts serve to illuminate the idea of the secure base **(the 5Rs):**

- **R**esponsiveness
- **R**elationship
- **R**eciprocity
- **R**outine, and
- **R**itual.

The **responsiveness** of the caregiver to the concerns and preferences of the young person may help to build a meaningful **relationship.** Apparently Marks and Spencer have a training slogan which states 'retail is in the detail'. If attention to detail by retail staff wins the trust and loyalty of shoppers, it may also be the case that attention to detail by carers may gradually win the trust and loyalty of the young person in care. The detail that matters may appear to involve items which on the surface seem somewhat strange. Food preferences, for example, may take on special significance in this context. The independent evaluator of the original Kent Family Placement Project, developed by Nancy Hazel and colleagues and which pioneered the placement of adolescents in Britain in the 1970s, noted this point.

> Adolescents themselves mentioned food as particularly significant, and the extent to which they felt Project families were ready to accommodate to unusual and perhaps (to them) bizarre eating preferences was a matter of great symbolic and practical importance to the adolescents. One wanted nothing but a particular brand of soup when she arrived at her placement: the foster mother promptly stocked up a cupboard full of tins so the adolescent could help herself whenever she wished; this evidence of care was very significant to the girl concerned.

(Yelloly, 1979, p.19)

Reciprocity in a relationship helps to build and sustain bonds of trust and commitment. If I do something for you and you do something for me in return, this sequence of mutual help brings us closer and builds a bond of commitment between us. This bond will grow stronger if the cycle of helping each other continues. Regular reassuring **routines** and the structure and symbolism of **ritual** represent order and predictability for a child whose life may have been very chaotic and lacking in much semblance of order. The structure of school routines may prove very supportive for a vulnerable child, the reassuringly familiar constancy of how the school day begins or ends; how certain classes are managed. Similarly, rituals around family, cultural, religious, school or community events may have deep meaning for a child whose life has lacked much structure or order.

Iain and Clive, foster carers of teenaged Ben, describe the stability they have been able to offer to Ben and the consequence of this.

> Ben has certainly moved on a lot from the teenager who first came to us. He's been let down a lot in his life and he'd come to expect that people would let him down, but he knows we won't do that. We feel the stability has been very important to him. He'd had some difficult foster placements, with carers who hadn't known what to do with a gregarious, gay young man who dyed his hair pink. With us he can be himself – we're not going to be shocked by what he does. And at the same time we can make it very clear when his behaviour isn't appropriate in a particular situation.

(Quoted in Bond (ed), 2005, p. 94)

Identity - knowing their story

Young people in care have a deep need to know who they are, to whom they belong, and to whom they are important: a set of questions whose answers lie in the concept of **identity**. All youngsters have to grapple with the issue of identity and who they are becoming. But for the youngster in care, questions of identity can be very raw indeed.

A young care leaver quoted in Biehal (1999) emphasises the importance of "knowing the score" about their family circumstances and why they are in care, even if the facts are painful. Ultimately the truth, properly digested, can contribute to healing and much more so than misguided attempts to shield the young person from reality. Hiding aspects of the truth introduces uncertainty and casts a shadow of doubt over the credibility, honesty and commitment of the adults implicated. Where the truth emerges after an extended period of deceit or cover up, there may well be a correspondingly long period of recovery and delay before the young person may, if ever, begin to feel secure in trusting what he or she is told.

Donald and his life story

Seven-year-old Donald, who was mycrocephalic and had multiple disabilities, would not be separated from his life story. He tore all other books but not this one. Although he could certainly not comprehend the story, he knew it was his. Because it was valued, he was proud of himself. He turned the pages carefully and pointed at the pictures and laughed.

(Case vignette in Argent and Kerrane, 1997, p.68)

It may be helpful to think of the child as having a hunger for the truth, a hunger that has to be assuaged. As with the bird which feeds its fledglings, adults feeding the truth to the child must ensure it is sufficiently digested to reflect the child's capacity to absorb it at a given time. Making the story digestible in this sense certainly does not mean distorting it. It means that the story must be told in a way that preserves its essence.

One way of trying to make sense of one's story is to tell it. Doing "life story work" is a well known technique that can usefully be employed by social workers and carers. This is well explained in a popular guide for adults doing such direct work with children (Ryan and Walker, 2007), as well as in a guide for children, which explains what life story work is and why it is important to do it (Shah and Argent, 2006). Life story work can help children piece together and understand the significance of events, relationships and people from their past, in order to help them come to terms with their identity and move confidently into the future.

Martin (1998) also gives a powerful example of how a specific research technique – transcribing onto the computer screen young Canadian care leavers' accounts of their transition from care to the "big world" – could have a positive impact on the young research participants. At least some found that trying to tell their story helped them to review, clarify and own it. Their story helped reinforce their identity and their sense of place in the world. Such "self-narrative" work might profitably be used by professionals who are working with young people in care, especially those in their teens or beyond.

> This is how I became me, today. Or at least how my perspective has been coloured. I was in a difficult situation, and then I got out of it and into another one, and so on, until I found the right place for me to be in. Where I feel I should belong is very far from where I began. I am now in a place that I didn't even know existed until I was about 15, but I now call it home. I don't know if it's modern society, or just society in general, but in my experience I have found it best to be able to make choice for yourself. Sometimes your original blood relatives may not know how to care for you as well as complete strangers. I will always love my parents, unconditionally. They are not bad people, just a little confused about themselves and how to raise their daughter. In that way, it is ironic that my godparents, who don't have any children, seem to be handling me better than my original parents. I guess because everything messed up when I was young, I was at the point where a lot could be damaged, and therefore a lot had to be fixed, which led to more complications.
>
> *(A précis of her story invited at the completion of the self-narrative process by the researcher from a young woman who had left care, in Martin, 1998)*

POINT TO CONSIDER

Consider how you might help a young person to write their story with your support (as a carer or social worker). It might help to do this with the aid of a computer, and might be especially appropriate with a young person who is comfortable with computers. In this approach, you and he or she sit at the computer together and you might do the typing while he or she starts telling you things about themselves. As you type, you would check back sentence by sentence that you have captured what he or she is trying to say.

Ethnic and religious identity

It is likely to be important for young people to have the opportunities to sustain and develop their ethnic and religious identities. For example, it may be important for them to have opportunities to celebrate religious and other festivals e.g. Chinese New Year (pictured), Divali, or Ramadan, to name a few, and to observe particular customs. For those children placed with carers from a similar ethnic or religious background, this will be relatively easy to do. For others not so placed, it will be important that the care arrangements are respectful of the values and expectations of the child's background and that efforts are made to help the child maintain a continuity and connection with cultural and religious traditions. As Argent and Kerrane (1997, p.70) put it: 'dietary laws, rules of hygiene and dress, traditions, rituals and festivals can draw people together or set them apart'.

Sue Jardine was adopted from Hong Kong and came to the UK at 18 months. Reflecting on her often painful, cultural experiences growing up in a transracial placement, she has some suggestions to help children growing up outside their culture. One is for children to have access to a cultural guide or mentor 'to explain about cultural festivals, to show them how to cook, or how to approach concerns such as hair or skin care' (Jardine, 1999, p.155). Zena Dickson (1995) had a black father and a white mother and spent time in foster care. She too emphasises the importance of helping the young person stay in touch with their culture.

For young people who have been placed transracially in foster care or adoptive families, meeting others with similar experiences can be a boost to their self-esteem, as Karen Moir points out.

> It was once I was away from home and at college, during my social work training, that I began to make friends with many people from various ethnic backgrounds. With the support of my friends, and through working with many different people, I was helped to develop a true sense of my own identity and to feel proud of who I am. It is an ongoing process that I continue to work through but now I know my ethnicity is not a problem, in fact it's an asset.

(Quoted in Harris (ed), 2006, p. 347)

If carers and social workers are to respond adequately and sensitively to the needs of children from minority ethnic communities, it is important they have sufficient information about the child's cultural background and the significance of such detail. Sumpton (1999) offers a very helpful framework for beginning to assemble an individual picture for each child.

Checklist for obtaining information on the black child

1 Country of origin, town/village; place of birth of child, parents and grandparents

2 Religion – community/sect; religious beliefs – pillars of faith, place of worship, holy book, religious law

3 Language(s) – written/spoken

4 Child-rearing practices: family traditions (e.g. circumcision, naming); health issues (e.g. use of herbal alternative medicine; blood test for sickle cell anaemia/ thalassaemia)

5 Customs/ceremonies (weddings, funerals, use of horoscopes, rituals)

6 Festivals celebrated

7 Food – diet often linked with religion

8 Dress/hair – clothes, appearance, tribal markings and jewellery

9 Adoption – whether legally sanctioned or permitted/recognised by religion

10 Other relevant issues such as hobbies

(Sumpton, 1999, p.89)

Our response to children's faith is also important.

> The black child's participation in the social life of their religion is as important as his or her involvement in festivals and celebrations in which they are often encouraged to participate ... for some black children, their involvement with a religious community could provide the stability, continuity and boundaries they need.
>
> *(Okitikpi 1999, p. 121)*

POINTS TO CONSIDER

How can carers and social workers maximise appropriate opportunities for young people to develop their ethnic and religious identity?

How can a child in care placed outside their culture be helped to stay in touch with their ethnic or religious background?

How can agencies best respond to carers' needs for advice and support in these matters?

Self-esteem

> Although feelings of self-worth and esteem form within early relationships, they need not remain fixed. It is within negative care-giving relationships

that low self-esteem becomes established, but later experiences of more positive relationships – at any age in the life-span – can help to improve poor self-concepts. People who take an interest, who listen, care and love us, make us feel better. They improve our self-image and bolster our self-esteem. Children who are not loved at home may nevertheless develop feelings of self-worth if a relative takes an interest, a teacher appears concerned and caring, or a residential worker responds with kindness and consistency.

(Howe et al, 1999, p.256)

Self-esteem grows from our sense of how we measure up to our own expectations and those of people important to us. Positive self-esteem is widely accepted as a valuable buffer against the adverse effects of negative experience. The child with good self-esteem will be less vulnerable in the face of negative events or processes in their lives. Good self-esteem derives from a sense of being accepted by people whose relationship one values and from a sense of accomplishment in tasks one values (Rutter, 1990). Acceptance in valued relationships and success in valued tasks can build self-esteem. It is important to note that accomplishment does not have to occur in a competitive or public setting. Accomplishing a private goal or a comparatively modest task privately conceived may help self-esteem. The achievement does not have to be momentous – it does not have to be along the lines of coming first in French in regional or national state exams. The accomplishment could amount to reliably and competently taking care of the school pet – low key but nevertheless an achievement.

A cautionary note

Self-esteem is a double-edged sword. Too little is debilitating. But too much may be harmful in another way. Unbridled self-esteem may make a person less than likeable in social relations. Overbearing self-esteem does not win many friends or influence people. It is important for self-esteem to be tempered with a sufficient degree of both self-awareness – a sense of how one comes across to other people – and empathy – a capacity to understand the other's point of view. Young people in care may be preoccupied with negative perceptions of themselves and the perceptions and motivations of others – based on prior negative experiences. They may be short of the accepting relationships and valued accomplishments that nurture self-esteem.

Self-efficacy

Ben, now a 19-year-old Australian, had experienced unstable public care since the age of three-and-a-half. Ben's story is instructive. His determination to succeed comes from within himself and his experience, but it is also supported by a girlfriend, a small circle of friends formed in school, the encouragement of former foster carers (who have also promised financial support for his planned business venture), and his contribution to an advocacy group for young people in care. His self-belief also sustained him in his struggle to get training and ultimately a job in his chosen field of technology. But as Ben's story underlines, self-efficacy may require not only personal qualities, but also supportive relationships and experiences.

> The main reason I want to start my own business is that I want to prove everybody (wrong) that said I am not going to make it, seeing that I've been in care, I am not going to do it because I am too dumb. I'm going to prove them wrong.

> *(Quoted in Maunders et al, 1999, p.53)*

Self-efficacy grows from experience. It is about qualities of optimism, persistence and "stickability" and believing that one's own efforts make a difference. One's sense of self-efficacy is enhanced by opportunities to practise the art of taking responsibility and taking or contributing to decisions which affect the minutiae or broader trend of one's life. In the case of young people enduring adversity in their lives, a healthy expression of self efficacy may be through some forms of resistance to the pressures on them.

> Music, sport, having a twin and being mischievous were the things that kept me sane. I loved playing the piano and practised for hours, often falling asleep with my head on the lid. Practice time was in a room on my own, where I composed, dreamed and scribbled down ideas. I kept this part of myself hidden for fear it would be stopped.

> Creativity has proved my saving grace. I've written songs dedicated to the girls from the homes and those who had their childhoods stolen.

> *(Evon Brennan, 2007, reflecting on surviving a tough regime of care)*

A cautionary note

Applying these ideas to work with children in care or in need does not mean, however, handing over decisions to young people. It is important to avoid some wholesale surrender of authority - and responsibility - from the adult carers to the young person. It must never be a question of the adult professional or carer seeking the views of the child or young person on some important issue regarding, for example, placement choice and merely endorsing the choice of the young person. As Gillian Schofield observes (1998, p.364), it is important to listen to the young person as *part* of a comprehensive and subtle assessment of their needs and circumstances, but also to remember that 'listening to children is a much more complicated process than simply obtaining a view from the child about where they want to live and with whom'.

POINTS TO CONSIDER

Encouraging responsibility

Can you remember times when you were younger when you were given responsibility to make decisions and you had to live with the consequences?

Can you think of some examples and who was involved and how?

What was it like to experience this degree of trust and to have to live with what you chose?

Recalling your memories and experience, what lessons would you draw for encouraging responsibility among young people in care?

Don't forget

Remember that the Department of Health Looking After Children (LAC) materials, and the way in which they are used, can provide excellent opportunities to assess and enhance the self-efficacy of young people in care.

Enhancing the self-efficacy of young people in care by helping them to work together

Young people in care can work together to support each other, to promote understanding of their needs, or to help others. This collective effort seems a promising way to foster self-efficacy in the individual participants. Young people in care can be involved, for example, in training exercises for social services staff (Department of Health, 1999, p.48); in making a film about their experience of life in care (Noon, 2000); in annual conferences for children in out-of-home care (Department of Health, 1999, p.47); in the development of a Children's Rights Handbook, or a video for those leaving care (O'Neale, 2000, p.41); or the organising of a fundraising cake sale for a local children's hospital (Gilligan, 1999, p.190).

A cautionary note

While it may be helpful and appropriate to work with groups of young people in care, it is important not to trap them within their "in care" identity and to render it a virtual condition of receiving support or recognition. We should also aim to help young people in care to move beyond "care". In the long run, it may be much more valuable and productive for the young person to make connections and friendships with young people who are not in care. This is not to dismiss the idea of having friends from care, but it is to raise concern about *only* having friends from care.

What promotes self-esteem and self-efficacy for a young person?

- Academic competence (especially as evidenced by early reading skills)
- Enjoyment of interests and hobbies which offer encouragement
- Respite when home life is difficult
- Joining in co-operative/team ventures
- Taking responsibilities consistent with their ability
- Helping others in need
- Supportive relationships

(Points derived from Werner and Smith, 1992, pp.204-5)

- High quality friendships (reciprocated "best friend" friendships) may help to raise self-esteem in children who have experienced chronic abuse or neglect.

(Bolger et al, 1998)

"Planful competence": Close to the idea of self-efficacy, the concept of "planful competence" refers to a capacity to plan and to avoid impulsive and unconsidered reactions to life's unfolding events (Clausen, 1991, cited in Rutter, 1999). It seems linked to more positive outcomes.

According to Quinton and Rutter (1988), this more planned approach to life may be encouraged by a number of factors:

- positive school experience, defined as two or more of: state examination success, positive view of school work or school peer relationships, or a 'positive recall of three or more areas of school life, including sport, responsibility, arts and craft and academic lessons' (p.164);

- feelings of self-worth;

- encouraging young people to believe that 'they can control what happens to them' (p.223); and

- imparting social problem-solving skills to the young people.

> You can't just leave them with a blank space. You've got to fill in the gaps so they understand . . . So you've got to listen to what the child wants and do it and if you can't do it you've got to tell them why, explain to them so they can understand. Otherwise they get confused and then it gets worse for them as they grow up . . . you know, whether it's good news or bad news, you've got to tell them . . . there may not be a good outcome, in my case there isn't, but I know why. And that's good enough, you know.

> *(Young person quoted in Biehal, 1999, p.87)*

© Digital Vision

A cautionary note

It is important to remember that each person's experience is unique and what works for one may not be relevant for another. It is especially important for somebody who has been through an experience that, on the surface, appears similar to another's, to avoid the trap of saying, 'I did it, so you can too'.

(For a further exploration of some of the concepts considered in this chapter and in Chapter 4, see Daniel *et al* (1999a) and Howe *et al* (1999).)

POINTS TO CONSIDER

Learning from your own experience

Looking back on your own childhood, adolescence and young adulthood:

- What were some of the formative experiences in your life (holidays, hobbies, sporting involvement, friendships)?

- What were critical experiences which now look to have been turning points in opening up new options, ideas or opportunities for you?

- Were there particular people at different times over the years who were influential in introducing you to new skills or interests or helped you to appreciate unrecognised or forgotten strengths or talents which you possessed? (Remember that people do not necessarily have to have been involved in your life for a long time to be particularly influential in this way.)

- Were there difficult times which you got through, either because of special support from particular people and/or special effort on your own part?

- Were there young people your own age who were helpful to you as you look back now? What did they do that was helpful? What was it about the way they related to you that you remember as being helpful and supportive?

- What lessons might you draw from your own helpful experiences growing up which MIGHT have relevance in your work with children in care?

4 Helping young people in care to "stay connected" to key people

I thought about what the word "contact" meant to me as a young person in care. It meant an opportunity to see the ones I loved, to exchange emotions and feelings, and to share memories. There are different types of contact, but whatever form it takes, to me it means the same as communication, as contact cannot take place without it.

(Dickson, 1995)

Keeping in touch

A key part of work with young people and of building on any potential they have for resilience is to help them stay connected to key figures in their lives or their past, that is, to members of their **social network** (see figure on p. 46). A young person's social network is a key resource in their social development. The people and relationships that make up that network are key potential sources of support both while they are in care, or when they go on to be adopted, or in the years after they leave care. Not all the relationships in the network may be positive. Some may be stressful and conflictual. Some people may exert a destructive influence in the young person's life. While it is true that negative as well as positive energy may flow through social network relationships, it is also the case that key streams of social support may flow through the network. Key members of the social network are typically parents and siblings. But there are also grandparents and aunts and uncles. There may also be non-relatives who may be important: friends, the parents of friends, neighbours, adults who play a mentoring role, such as a teacher, a sports coach, drama instructor, a faith leader, or adults who have been enlisted in a helping capacity by social services on a voluntary or paid basis.

The significance of network or family members

Debbie Hindle (1998) highlights the significance of network members in enhancing the resilience of Kennie, a teenage boy working through the impact on him and his family of his mother's psychiatric illness.

> His [Kennie's] growing ability to turn to his father for help has proved an important step towards Kennie developing independence . . . The wider extended family - grandparents, uncles, cousins - has taken on a greater importance for Kennie, who was recently the only member of his nuclear family to attend a cousin's wedding. He enjoyed the event and described how it made him feel better - there were other people who he could look up to, a wider family of which he could feel part . . . For Kennie, his growing interest in language, in poetry and literature, as well as consistent support from his teachers, opened an unexpected door to his inner world.

> (Hindle, 1998, pp.263-4)

In the case of children in public care, their network may also include current or past carers who have struck up a meaningful relationship with the young person, or indeed relatives of the carers. As Andersson (1999) puts it, in work with children in care our concept of the young person's "family" has to be broadened.

While an impressive range of research backs the value of contact with parents for children in care, there are some dissenting or at least sceptical voices (Quinton *et al*, 1997). There may be some circumstances where parental contact with one or both parents may not be desirable. But even where this applies, the value of, for example, sibling and grandparental contact should not be overlooked. Keeping some such connections to family alive may prove very important later on as the young person strives to make their way in the world as a young adult. The reality for young people in care is that many professional relationships are transient, however much the "system" may wish it to be otherwise. Social workers may come and go over the course of a young person's extended career in care. There may be perfectly legitimate reasons for such frequent changes, but it is undeniable that such changes fly in

the face of the child's need for consistency and reliability. Carers, too, may chop and change for all kinds of reasons: illness, retirement, emigration, placement changes precipitated by the young person's behaviour, or a change in agency policy that closes down a residential setting. Ironically, it may be members of the very family with its problems from which the young person sought to escape, or from which social services sought to protect, who may constitute the only set of constant figures for the young person as he or she grows up.

In stressing the value of family members, the benefits of links with supportive non-relatives should not be discounted either. Since young people growing up in care risk having smaller enduring networks than other young people, it is important to preserve and expand networks where at all possible. For the young person in foster care, foster relatives may be important. Rashid (2000) cites an example from his small study of black foster carers of Darren who became close to one of the carer's granddaughters, and of Amy who identified with her carer's eldest daughter. For a number of children in Rashid's study, visits to the extended family of the foster carers in the Caribbean or in other countries had been a decisive positive turning point in the young person's progress in the placement. Foster relatives may also become meaningful network members into the future (Andersson, 1999). A foster grandparent might, for example, become a confidant outside the family of origin, or offer holidays or lodgings when the young person reaches 18 years of age (Hazel, 1981, p.101). Rashid (2000) notes how Amy, who fell out with her foster carers and left them, had now, some years later, mended her fences with them, to the extent that her daughter is considered a granddaughter of the foster carers. This is yet another example from Rashid of the generously inclusive nature of caring in many black families.

It is worth remembering that different family or network members may assume different meanings or significance at different stages. McTeigue (1998) reports that children in her study of ten foster children varied by age in terms of their interest in contact with parents. Meetings with parents seemed to be regarded almost as a chore by the younger (primary school age) children, whereas such meetings and contact were seen positively by the older teenage children. In a 15-year follow-up study of 20 young children in long-term care in Sweden, Andersson (1999) noted a tendency for more interest to be shown in contact with biological fathers as the young people grew older. Overall, this is an important message – strongly-held views may change or mellow with the passage of time. Adults with responsibility need to bear this in mind. They need to serve as wise stewards for the child of information and connections at their disposal.

Keeping links with family alive does not have to mean that the young person has to return home. There are actually three options rather than two, in relation to links with family in after care: to not go home, to go home for good or for a while, or to stay in touch. For many young people, the third seems to have much appeal. Relatives may be valued members in a young person's social network. What most young people in care need in terms of social support is 'defence in depth' (Sinclair and Gibbs, 1998, p.76); the more members there are in their social network, the more likely they may be able to access social support when they need it. As Sinclair and Gibbs observe in relation to children in residential care:

> A system which provides them with a variety of adults to whom to turn is less likely to fail them than a system in which they are dependent on one.

(p.245)

Promoting contact

There is at least some evidence that, in terms of the social functioning and development of a young person in care, it may be more significant for them to have positive feelings towards their parents than merely to have contact alone. This underlines the complexity of what is involved in promoting and supporting contact. The subtle (or not so subtle) messages about parents which carers and social workers may give off, even unconsciously, may influence a child's perception of their parents. Also, it becomes clear that what happens in the visit or contact may colour the views children hold of their parents. An enjoyable relaxed occasion sharing some activity may leave better memories and views than a stilted and formal encounter in, for example, an alien office environment. For contact to be meaningful and successful on an ongoing basis, it may be important for the child and parent to share enjoyable experiences in the contact. Otherwise, the separation which defines their relationship robs them of something in common to share.

Possible activities for children to share with their birth parents in contact

Shopping expeditions
Visits to the park
Visits to the zoo
Visits to the playground
Visits to the public library
Car rides
Country walks

(from Argent and Kerrane, 1997, p.74)

Here are some other ideas:

Going to the hairdresser together
Going to a sporting event together
Going shopping together to buy something for the young person
Going to a funfair together

Some examples of simple ideas and good practice in relation to contact and access

One workshop participant offered the wonderfully simple and effective suggestion of buying a jar of blowing bubbles for non-threatening and non-demanding entertainment and distraction during a contact session involving a younger child.

A unit head of an adolescent unit recalled a tense contact visit by a father with a very troubled relationship with his son, who was ambivalent about the visit. Previous incidents had necessitated the presence of a social worker and a plainclothes policeman. The boy needed a haircut – something the father pointed out. Thinking quickly and spotting the opportunity for a normal father and son activity, the unit head suggested to the father that they all go to the hairdressers for a haircut! The outing was a success, and a great deal more relaxed and good-humoured than if they had all remained cooped up in the visitors' room of the residential unit.

A carer family lived near the sea and owned a beach hut at a local resort. They spent a good deal of time each summer at the beach hut. Contact visits often took place at the beach hut and the whole informal and fun atmosphere meant they were a lot more enjoyable and productive.

A mother whose mental health difficulties meant she could not have full responsibility for her child still wanted to play a regular part in her life. One way she did this was to prepare a meal for her daughter whenever the girl came to visit her as part of the contact arrangements. Sharing the meal and its preparation became a practical and symbolic expression of caring by the mother and an enriching experience and future memory for the child.

The importance of family and networks

Two extracts below illustrate the importance of family – immediate and extended – for young people when they leave care.

> The majority of children and adolescents who are separated return to parents or the wider family once they leave care. The majority of these reunions occur in spite of the reasons for entering care or the length of time away. Even young adults, some convicted of grave offences, long separated from home, periodically rest in the bosom of their families, once professionals have ceased their ministrations. As we abandon the task, it is usually the family, frequently identified as damaging or deficient, which takes up the role of main supporter of children and adolescents. Young people may not stay long at home, they may use the family as a springboard or a bolthole from outside excitements, they may return swiftly because all else fails or because they exhaust the tolerance of other benefactors. But, parents and the wider family, probably deficient on many criteria, are a resource which could be enhanced by social work support and encouragement.
>
> (Bullock et al, 1993, p.229)

... for some of the young people, their extended family was their *primary* [emphasis in original] source of support: aunts, uncles, siblings, grandparents or step-parents all had an important role to play. Siblings were a particularly important source of emotional support and for some of the young people their closest and most supportive relationships were with brothers and sisters. For a few young women, their relationships with older sisters had a parental quality and they would rely on them for support, advice and guidance. Some young people had been cared for by members of their extended family and had developed close bonds with them, seeing them as additional or surrogate parental figures. A few had lived with grandparents at some stage in their lives and maintained a positive relationship with them, which they found helpful. For others, contact with siblings, grandparents, aunts, uncles, cousins did not offer clear practical support but it fulfilled an important symbolic role for young people who sought contact with extended family members to meet their need for a sense of belonging and identification with their families. However, for young people who had suffered severe parental rejection, this identification with the wider family could not fully meet their need.

(Biehal, 1999, p.131, discussing the experience of care leavers in her and her colleagues' studies in terms of contact with relatives and extended family)

Positive relationships with network members (relatives, friends and others) are important for young people in care for a number of reasons. Network members can serve as:

- a source of social support day to day;

- a source of advocacy on behalf of the young person;

- a point of contact and support when the young person leaves care, and/or in the first year or two afterwards;

- a source of contacts for job, training or leisure opportunities;

- a source of affirmation of social, cultural and genealogical identity;

- a source of information and mementoes about personal history;

- a source of culturally appropriate role models;

- a source of mentoring and encouragement in educational progress;

- a source of consolation, whether practical or symbolic, when times are hard;

- a source of accommodation in a crisis;

- a source of opportunities to address some of the emotional pain associated with the reasons for having to be in local authority care in the first place; and

- a source of symbolic reassurance that there is indeed someone to call on or someone to whom one is important, or with whom one can identify (Biehal, 1999). Whether such expectations would survive being tested is actually beside the point. Much social support is derived from the perception that such support is available or can be called upon.

Contact with birth parents may have positive and often hidden spin-offs in lots of ways. The values and priorities which parents hold dear may be a source of inspiration for young people in care. This young man's mother ultimately died as a result of her addiction, but as he observes:

> We always knew she loved us and she cared very much about our education whenever she wasn't drinking.

> *(Quoted in Ajayi and Quigley, 2006, p. 68)*

The specific value of sibling relationships

While their relationships may often be complex and further complicated by family stresses and conflicts, siblings are likely to remain very important for young people in the care system. Siblings understand, like no-one else perhaps, the pressures of growing up within the family of origin. They may be able to help make sense of obscure details of personal history. They may be able to offer practical help and advice, now and in the future. When parents and social workers and others who know the young person's background are dead or disappeared, siblings may be the only ones left with an understanding of the young person's history and experience and a special commitment to helping them.

The reality, however, is that pathways into and through care often separate and distance siblings from each other. It is important that carers and social workers are alert to the deep meaning and longer-term significance of sibling ties for youngsters in care.

What can carers do to promote positive ties between siblings who are living apart?

- Organise outings for the siblings together

- Have a routine of regular overnight stays in each other's houses

- Organise regular participation in a shared activity (e.g. horse riding)

- Arrange shared holidays

- Encourage the sharing of each other's celebrations (birthdays, religious rites of passage)

- Offer invitations to non-resident siblings to stay over at Christmas or other periods of cultural/religious significance (Rashid, 2000)

- Take photographs of them together often

- Organise joint visits to significant places from their past – the graves of close relatives, hospitals where they were born, houses where they lived for significant periods, schools they went to together, people who cared for them together

- Arrange joint meetings with significant adults in their social network

- Encourage regular phone contact

- Encourage regular letter writing, text messaging or emailing

- Organise a shared family storybook that seeks to capture their common history

- Record videos of shared activities together

POINTS TO CONSIDER

In what ways could you promote productive links with siblings for children in foster care based on your own experience or ideas?

Thinking of a specific case, what needs to be done to strengthen ties between siblings and who needs to agree to how to do this?

Friends and peers

> Along with knowing whether or not children have friends, we must know who their friends are and the quality of their relationships with them.
>
> (Hartup, 1996, p.10)

> It is particularly vital not to view peers as largely negative influences. Children help each other a great deal and all adults should be aware of friends and age-mates as actual or potential resources for resolving difficulties.
>
> (Hill, 1999, p.143)

It is important not to underestimate the value of friendships and peer relationships in terms of social support and developmental progress. Yet being in care may hinder friendships.

How may being in care affect children's friendships?

- Coming into care (or moving placements) may break up friendships since the child may have to move some distance to live with the new carers.

- Since friendship, especially in younger people, requires contact to be sustained, enforced distance may cause friendships to wither.

- New carers consciously or unconsciously may discourage links with the past.

- Travel time and costs may also be a barrier.

- The child's in-care identity may make it difficult for them to form new friendships with children not in care.

- There may be barriers to such friendships, such as staff screening of contacts, or house rules about visitors which the young person does not find congenial.

- Child protection procedures may also be an issue, affecting, for example, spontaneous plans to stay over at one another's houses.

- There may also be more subtle inhibitions – the child's sense of stigma or embarrassment about being in care, or their uncertainty about how to explain or describe their care status.

- Children may thus feel more at ease forming friendships with children in the same boat who do not need explanation or deception about the facts surrounding being in care.

- Children may become trapped in a ghetto of care relationships, literally only having contact with children (living) or adults (working) in care. This risks leaving them open to social isolation on leaving the care system. As one young person puts it starkly: 'I won't have any friends when I leave care' (quoted in Page and Clarke, 1977, p.54).

POINTS TO CONSIDER

Friendships and their importance

Think of one young person in care whom you know. Who are their friends? How were these friendships formed and what do they mean to the young person? What keeps them going? Could the friendship be "helped" in any way (a very delicate art!)?

When children move placement, what can carers and social workers do to help children's friendships to survive the move?

Peer relations with other young people in care

Ruth Emond, who spent long periods in two residential units studying the lives and worlds of the young residents, reminds us how important the world of the young people and their relationships may be. She quotes a young person with whom she spoke to illustrate her point:

> At the end of the day you only have each other. The staff are lovely but they're paid to be here and there's no getting out of that. They can't be with us every minute so it's up to us to make the place home . . . make sure

LIBRARY, UNIVERSITY OF CHESTER

it's the way we want it . . . no one is allowed to get too big for their boots here . . . it just spoils it for everyone. The staff cannae stop that happening, that's for us to do.

(Bryony, quoted in Emond, 2002, p. 38)

Important methods and mechanisms in identifying and connecting with social network members

Three approaches may be useful to consider: **life story work**; the use of a **social network map**; or use of an **eco-map**. Life story work (Ryan and Walker, 2007) using photographs of people in the network and photos of moments from the young person's earlier life gathered from network members can play an invaluable role.

Through their life books, the children involved may come to own their story little by little, mainly because they have gone through them so often with other people and each time it comes clearer to them. Besides, in retelling it, they think of new questions to ask and gain new realisations each time.

Example of a social network map

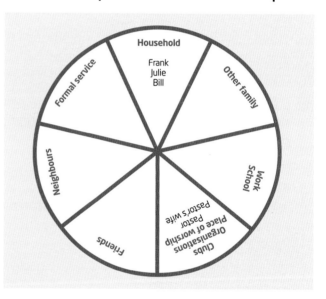

Example of an ecomap

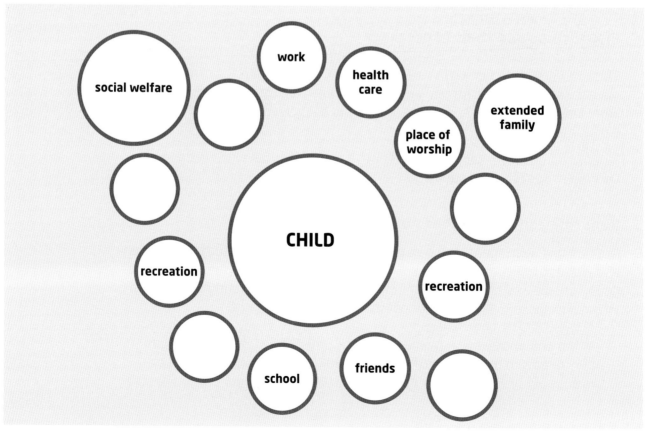

5 Getting the most out of school opportunities and experiences

© Reportdigital

I am a 17-year-old girl, and I have been accommodated for four years, during which time I moved 22 times, across four regional divisions. As a result my schooling has been quite messed about . . . However, unlike a great many young people I returned to school . . . I had a particularly good relationship with one teacher . . . I was also very lucky to have incredibly strong support from the staff in the home who cajoled, conned and coerced me back into school. They kept telling me that I could succeed and made me believe it.

(Young woman in care who received encouragement from staff in the home to return to school, quoted in Sinclair, 1998, p.22)

Why school is important for young people in care

> School life, with its rich environment of new relationships and tasks, presents children with occasions to identify, develop and establish fresh, more robust and socially valued aspects of the self.
>
> *(Howe et al, 1999, p.260)*

School can offer many opportunities to young people in the care system and play a central role in personal and social development. Quite apart from its specific educational role, school may offer a whole host of opportunities that help to support the social development of the young person in care. School may:

- be a source of friendships and peer relationships;

- serve as an asylum from other painful arenas in the young person's life;

- offer meaningful roles as student in the classroom or in extra-curricular activities;

- offer very precious "normal" activities and experiences separate from the world of "care";

- provide opportunities for supportive or mentoring relationships with concerned teachers or other school staff;

- help develop social skills;

- build self-esteem and self-efficacy;

- help the young person earn affirmation for school achievements from valued adults in the child's social network.

- offer a gateway to the world of work;

- help establish life-long interests and hobbies;

- offer an alternative source of counselling and support with personal problems;

- provide "turning point" experiences for the young person as they develop.

The value of positive school experiences

Quinton and Rutter (1988) found that positive school experiences seemed to be connected to a later capacity to approach decisions about work and marriage on a planned basis. This is very significant given the heightened risk of powerlessness and passivity which may be the legacy of life in care and the factors leading to it.

In a similar vein, a long-term follow-up study of women who had experienced sexual abuse when young found that positive school experiences (academic, sporting or extra-curricular) helped to

Potential school-based supports for educational progress and commitment

Career guidance
Computer-based tutorials
Extra-curricular activities
Home school liaison
Library (community)
Library (school)
One-to-one volunteer-paired-reading
Pastoral care tutoring
Peer tutoring
Supervised study
Temporary individual classroom assistant

distinguish those who had done better in terms of recovery (Romans *et al*, 1995).

An important dimension of positive school experiences is laying down positive memories of school and learning. Even if the young person chooses not to continue at school when legally eligible, or does not succeed as they wish, it may be important that the young person retains a positive impression of school, of teachers as approachable and likeable, and of learning as enjoyable and beneficial. Later in life, opportunities may open up and those positive impressions, if laid down earlier, may help to encourage the (older) young person to "take the plunge" back into education – a point made by researchers Sacker and Schoon (2007), who have studied the importance of second chance education in the subsequent lives of vulnerable youngsters. So success may not just be what we see right now in terms of positive results, but also in terms of the less obvious doors we help to keep open for a young person coming back into education at a later point in their life path.

In a recent study examining the emotional well-being of unaccompanied asylum-seeking young people (Chase *et al*, 2008), the authors offer the following examples of two young women for whom a combination of the support they were receiving and their own determination to do well, led to their success.

> Nadine had arrived in the UK at the age of 15, completed nine GCSEs in a single academic year ('I used to stay after school, like up to 7.30 in the evening, and do my coursework'), successfully completed four "AS" levels and then three "A" levels with high grades. At the time of the research, she was completing her first year of a Psychology degree at university. Nanu had arrived from Eritrea aged 16 and six months pregnant after having been raped by soldiers in Eritrea. She organised access to childcare provision herself through Care2Learn (the social worker had not known about this service), completed an ESOL (English as a second language) class in one year and at the time of her participation in the research was about to complete a three-year BTEC course in computing. Her son was by now four years old and she was applying to go to university to complete a degree in computer studies.

(Chase et al, *2008, p. 91)*

The importance of teachers

Teachers have as their main duty the promotion of learning, but they may also sometimes offer important psychological support at critical stages in the life of a child in care. Anne, at the age of 20, recalled how, when living abroad with her

Parameters of school performance

Attendance
Behaviour
Examination results
Homework
Motivation
Peer relationships

Dimensions of educational experience

Academic attainment
Non-academic attainment
Participation in school peer groups
Identification with the school as an institution
Relationships with individual teachers and other staff members
Engagement with extra-curricular activities
Avoidance of bullying

foster carers, a set of teachers had helped her at a troubled time in an isolated foster placement that subsequently broke down. The help and attention they offered had a positive effect: she took some exams which she passed and which helped boost her morale (see p. 62).

Fergus reminds us the difference the interest and belief of a particular teacher may make in the life of a vulnerable young person.

> You've got to find a teacher that has faith in you. I was a lazy sod. I used to sleep through most of my classes . . . There was one teacher who paid me in particular lots of attention . . . I liked her, she was very nice. She was the only one who ever had any confidence in me, all the other teachers used to blank me . . . She was my English teacher and she helped me pass my exam. That made me think that I could pass other exams and I had the same chance as anybody else . . . You've got to believe in yourself.
>
> *(Fergus, young boy in residential care quoted in Emond, 2002a, p. 31)*

Teachers can inspire confidence and they can offer support, as Claire recounts.

> My guidance teacher, I get on really well with her. She gives you help and advice. She's like your best friend in school. It was a big change from my last school and I didn't think I'd be able to do as well as I have. I'm sure I wouldn't have been able to do it without all the support I've got.
>
> *(Claire, quoted in Happer et al, 2006, p. 30)*

Susan, an adoptive mother of four, recalls how a particular head teacher and the stability of having the same class teacher helped her daughter Zoë, who was doing 'appallingly' at school. Zoë was five and had had no pre-school education. She had been placed in a special needs class at a school at which she had a teacher who was very inexperienced and negative about Zoë and Zoë's abilities. They then decided to change school, and Susan describes the effect that this had.

> 'The new school was much better,' Susan explains. 'When we met the head teacher, he said, "Let's not worry about what they're capable of. Let's wait until they're happy and running into school smiling and then see what happens." It was such an understanding attitude.' The new school was much smaller and Zoë had the same teacher for three years, which gave her stability.
>
> *(Quoted in Sturge-Moore (ed), 2005, p. 117)*

The experience of vulnerable young people not in care may also illuminate the valuable things teachers can do.

Yeah, Miss T., she's a good teacher. She's good to get along with in the mornings. Like if I'm feeling upset or something, as soon as I walk in the door and she says 'Hello' it just makes me happy. Just her being there.

(Amber – 14-year-old girl, quoted in Johnson, 2008)

My teacher is important because he's the one that urges me on to do stuff. He says, 'Come on Christopher, you can do it, just think positive', and if it wasn't for him I couldn't have done all of this that I have.

(Chris – 11-year-old boy, quoted in Johnson, 2008)

Based on his longitudinal study of how relations with teachers may impact on vulnerable children's resilience, Johnson (2008) emphasises the importance of children feeling "listened to" by their teachers, and suggests that such listening 'is one of the most basic ways teachers convey their respect for their students as fellow human beings'. He also identifies a number of other ways in which teachers may enhance resilience in their students based on the evidence of his study.

- 'They make themselves available and accessible to students.

- They engage students by actively listening to their concerns and worries.

- They take responsibility for actively teaching their students the basic reading, writing and numeracy skills needed for independent learning, even if their students have struggled in the past to master these skills.

- They have empathy with, and understanding of, their students' "tough" circumstances yet provide them with positive strategies to deal with adversity.

- They advocate for their students by mobilising existing support provisions that are available for "at risk" students.

- They actively use their power as adults and professionals to identify and oppose bullying and harassment at school; and finally,

- They remember the "human touches" that promote pro-social bonding between teachers and students'.

(Johnson, 2008, p. 395)

The importance of carers

Carers may also play a critical role in creating conditions that encourage and support educational progress.

> ... [the foster carers] prioritised my education. They spent endless hours at the kitchen table with my algebra book, bought numerous bottles of paint for art projects (only to later discover their new kitchen carpet speckled with blue dots!), joined in my chanting of French vocab on the way to school in preparation for my tests ... This year I will graduate from the University of Birmingham with a BA in Modern Languages.
>
> *(Fostered young person, quoted in Stadler, 2007, p. 12)*

The potential value of social experiences at school

> Most of the protective experiences at school for the ex-care girls did not involve academic successes. This serves to remind us that schooling constitutes a rich source of social experiences as well as an instrument for academic instruction.
>
> *(Quinton and Rutter, 1988, p. 223)*

Foundation academic competencies

Reading
Writing
Numeracy
Computer skills

Foundation social and survival competencies – a possible list

Boiling an egg
Cooking simple meals
Cycling
Driving
Learning and understanding basic budgeting
Learning constructive ways of dealing with anger and conflict
Learning safe approaches to alcohol and drugs
Making a simple shopping expedition
Making transactions using an Automatic Teller Machine (ATM)
Paying a bill
Saving money in a bank account
Sending text messages
Swimming
Understanding the basics of nutrition
Understanding the basic principles of safe sex and contraception
Using a telephone
Using the internet
Washing laundry in a washing machine

How and why being in care may affect school performance

> Several children were unable to recall exactly how many schools they had attended and a girl living in one home proudly opened her wardrobe to reveal the splendid mauves, greens, blues and greys of four brand-new uniforms of schools she had attended during the previous year.
>
> *(Berridge, 1985, p.116)*

- The problems that led to going into care may have adversely affected the young person's prior school attendance, motivation and behaviour. These difficulties may have established patterns of disengagement or delayed progress (e.g. reading problems) which may be difficult to dislodge.

- Being placed in care often means moving school and thereby losing contact with valued teachers and friends (McAuley and Trew, 2000) and possibly with school sports teams or other activity groups.

- Moving school also means having to relate to new teachers and new peers.

- A new placement may also mean changes in familiar routines (travel times, travel routes, mealtimes, timetables, etc) throughout the school day.

- Placement in care may also raise awkward feelings of difference for the young person at school (Freeman *et al*, 1996), at an age when children and young people are more likely to crave conformity with what they see as the expectations of peers.

- It may also raise questions for the young person about how to deal with probing by new peers about their in-care status.

- Educational needs and problems may come low down on the list of priorities of social workers and carers who are focused instead on social and behavioural problems.

- The status of being in care may mean that teachers and other adults have lower expectations of a young person's educational performance and potential.

- Educational problems may thus have become more embedded and intractable by the time the spotlight of attention is turned on them.

- Young people newly arrived in a school and without connections already in the school may be especially vulnerable to bullying.

Key people and roles in the life of the school

Art teacher
Caretaker/janitor
Chaplain
Cook
Form/class teacher
Gardener
Guidance counsellor
Music teacher
Nurse
PE teacher
Principal
Religion teacher
Subject teachers
Secretary
Year Head
Vice-Principal

- In the hurly-burly of planning and executing a move - often under pressure or in a hurry - not enough key information may be gathered from parents, any previous carers and teachers about educational history, performance and motivation.

An education plan

It is suggested that a key mechanism for securing the optimal educational progress of the young person in care lies in the development of an educational plan for each young person. The plan would address a number of issues. It would first recognise the importance of the aspects of educational experience beyond the narrowly academic, as illustrated in the list of key dimensions below. The aim of an educational plan must be to seek satisfactory outcomes on each of these dimensions in the young person's school experience.

In considering academic attainment, it seems important to have a broad view of what is desirable by way of attainment for the young person in care. Perhaps it is helpful to think of key competencies that it is desirable for a young person to master for his or her future as citizen and worker. While the school may have a clearer lead role in relation to academic competencies, it may also be helpful for teachers to be alert to opportunities to support young students in care to acquire key social competencies.

In preparing and evaluating an educational plan for a young person in care, it is important to have an accurate picture that reflects the young person's progress on key fronts.

School is an environment rich with potential relationships and opportunities to stimulate the social and academic development of the student. One of the challenges is ensuring that all the stakeholders remain alert to the range of people and roles offering potential educational supports within and without the school, and of physical settings within or linked to the school premises which may serve as an arena within which progress can occur.

> One boy became very close to the school janitor because he was kept in so often at breaks. She took an interest in him and has kept in contact with him since he moved from that school.
>
> (Daniel et al,1999b, p.8)

AN EDUCATION PLAN FOR A CHILD IN CARE – PROPOSALS FOR A FRAMEWORK

An effective plan

- Specifies the values/principles on which the plan is grounded, and to which the key players sign up (school, carers, social workers, social services, child)

- Identifies the young person's academic strengths and interests

- Acknowledges the young person's vulnerabilities (and keeps them in proportion)

- Identifies specific deficits which need remedy, e.g. reading delay, and specifies how these are to be tackled (e.g. special one-to-one tuition, paired reading opportunities, etc.)

- Summarises relevant information about educational progress and needs, as gathered from the child, current and former teachers, carers and any other relevant sources

- Identifies a strategy for handling any behavioural issues which may arise in the child's day in school (including the accessing of any extra support resources required)

- Clarifies responsibilities between social worker and carers for day-to-day liaison with the school

- Identifies school-based and external adult relationships supportive of educational and social development within school, and in particular seeks to identify an "educational mentor" for the young person

- Identifies opportunities for the young person to carry appropriate responsibility within the life of the school

- Considers the quality of the young person's school peer relationships and their implications for educational progress and participation in the life of the school

- Considers whether the young person is being victimised through bullying and how this might be addressed effectively (it should be noted that there is evidence that young people in care are more susceptible to being bullied than youngsters not in care (Daly and Gilligan, 2005).

- Reviews the young person's participation in extra-curricular and non-academic activities and needs and possibilities in this regard

- Specifies an explicit pastoral care strategy for the youngster (including roles of key teachers, format of contact, key issues for pastoral care agenda)

- Identifies likely optimal, moderate and poor educational outcomes based on current factors and patterns of performance and identifies pre-conditions/ factors likely to be associated with each level of outcome

- Assesses the young person's access to necessary educational supports, for example:
    - opportunities for paired reading for readers needing help
    - books at home for reading for pleasure
    - computer and educational software
    - homework support
    - opportunities to have stories/books read aloud by adult for enjoyment of (younger) child – valuable in terms of child receiving attention, stimulation of imagination, and encouragement of interest in reading
    - opportunities to listen to storytellers
    - involvement in local library
- Specifies outcomes sought for this month, term, academic year and end of projected education
- Considers the educational support needs which carers may have in terms of advice from teachers/educational psychologists, previous carers, etc.

Example of a school network

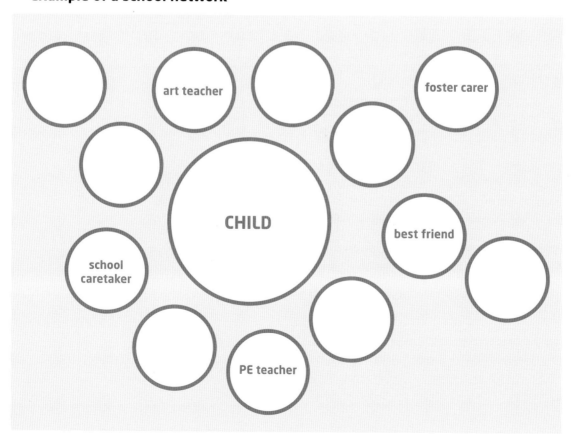

POINTS TO CONSIDER

The impact of school

What can be done to ensure that school and educational issues are placed very high up on the agenda when children come into care, and when placement changes occur?

What extra help may a youngster in care need to avoid the educational risks posed by moving placements?

Should schools and teachers have full information about a young person's history and progress?

How should a social worker strike the balance between a young person's understandable preference for privacy and a school's understandable wish to be granted information commensurate with its central role in the young person's daily life and development?

Which information should be shared with which types of teaching staff? How should the young person be involved in this process?

What extra supports and services might be appropriate to offer a school to help integrate a young person in care who presents with special behavioural problems or educational needs?

What might help to improve working relationships between schools and social workers, and schools and carers of children in care?

How can youngsters in care be protected from the risk of bullying at school?

Getting the most out of education

What conditions can help young people to get the most they can out of their education?

- Schools are as carefully assessed and selected for the child in care as for any child.

- Educational policy makers give a clear message that children in care are a priority group whose needs must be served appropriately. The social services department or equivalent recognises and emphasises that providing and supporting good educational experience are key elements of good care.

- Schools themselves also play their part in ensuring the satisfactory progress of young people in care on their rolls.

- Accurate and comprehensive information on educational progress is used to inform decision-making forums (courts, case conferences, case reviews) concerned with any young person in or possibly entering public care.

- Carers see that progress in school is one of the key issues with which they must deal each day.

- Schools are briefed appropriately by carers and social workers on relevant previous and current developments in the young person's life. Social workers and carers need to agree the division of responsibility in relation to this and to be sure that they fully respect the child's wishes and right to optimal privacy. This may mean negotiating carefully (and tactfully) with the school about the importance of information being shared only with certain key school personnel and under strict conditions of confidentiality.

- The young person has access to adequate space for study (desk, quiet area, etc) and appropriate homework support (a carer with interest and relevant knowledge – or access to someone who has).

- Extra-curricular interests and talents are encouraged.

- Social workers and carers have specific training opportunities in educational support for young people in care.

- Social services and education management offer the school and relevant teachers the resources, supports and incentives to engage with the needs of the child within and outside the classroom. This may sometimes require an additional teacher or teacher's assistant to be assigned to support the teacher in work with the child in an integration phase or to free up the class teacher to spend some time with the newcomer.

Setting in school for social/ educational opportunities and experiences

Art room
Assembly Hall
Canteen
Chaplaincy
Classroom
Cloakroom
Computer room
Corridor
Counsellor's room
Craft room
Garden
Gymnasium
Home room
Kitchen for cookery classes
Language laboratory
Library
Offices
Oratory
Playground
School bus
Science room
Sports field
Sports hall
Tuck-shop
Walk to school
Woodwork room
Workshop

Protective factors which may lead to later educational success for children in care

- Stability and continuity in care arrangements.

- Reading competence (learning to read early and being a fluent reader).

- A parent/carer who values education and sees it as a means to doing well in life.

- Friends outside care who do well at school.

- Out-of-school interests and hobbies (these help build social skills and contacts with adults and young people outside the care system).

- A significant adult who offers consistent encouragement and support and serves as a mentor and positive role model.

- Attending school regularly.

(Above points from Jackson and Martin, 1998, p.578)

How carers can help with the educational progress of a young person in care

- Have an authoritative parenting style (warm, firm and with high expectations) (NB This seems true for certain, but not necessarily all, cultures).

- Have contact with school about the child.

- Attend parent–school events/meetings.

- Show strong commitment to the value of education.

- Value effort.

- Expect and encourage the child to succeed academically.

- Monitor and help with homework.

(Above points from Masten and Coatsworth, 1998)

Principles in supporting young people in residential care to (re-) integrate into mainstream school

(These are applicable also to foster care.)

Mutual respect between carers and teachers
Clear philosophy about the importance of education
Attention to detail
A culture and daily routine within the care setting which clearly values education
Joint planning between carers and school
Determination in the face of setbacks
(Above points from Lindsay and Foley, 1999)

Alerting school to bullying or tension in peer relationships around ethnic identity (from Rashid, 2000)

POINTS TO CONSIDER

How carers can help

Does your agency offer training or support to foster carers in how to motivate and support young people in relation to educational progress and problems?

Are carers given information on how schools work and teachers think so that they can communicate and advocate effectively on behalf of the foster child in their care?

Are carers adequately briefed on the disciplinary code and pastoral care system of the schools to which they will relate specifically?

Are they given guidance on techniques and routines to support reading progress? Are they coached, for example, in effective paired reading techniques?

Are they given appropriate advice on other educational matters by someone appropriately qualified in teaching and familiar with the daily realities of foster care?

Are educational issues considered in matching carers and children?

Specific points for foster and residential carers

- Show interest in educational progress.
- Attend school events.
- Encourage reading for pleasure.
- Provide regular access to books for enjoyment and study.
- Link the young person to the local library.
- Act as advocate for the young person's educational needs with social workers and service managers.
- Secure career guidance that is not pitched too low in terms of expectations.
- Ensure ready access to key text books.
- Value any adult relationship for the young person that offers educational mentoring (or provide this time and listening oneself).
- Offer the right balance of stimulation and discipline for educational progress.
- Provide suitable quiet space for homework.
- Insist that placement moves are sensitive to minimum disruption in the school year.
- Encourage the young person to take responsibility and make decisions.
- Ensure that after-care plans make detailed and realistic provision to support educational progress (Jackson and Martin, 1998).

SCHOOL ACTIVITIES

Some examples of where and how a young person in care or in need might be able to contribute to school life and thereby develop a greater sense of belonging

Arts festival
Band/orchestra
Choir
Clubs
Community service
Debating society
Disco
Drama
Exhibitions of students' creative work
Fundraising projects for charity
Holidays
Mentoring younger students
Music
National/regional competitions (art, performance, music, science, debating, mathematics, essay writing, etc.)
Photographic club
School animals
School company
School float in community parade
School garden
School newspaper
School radio station
School shop
Sport
Social awareness projects
Trips
Twinning activities with schools abroad (video-conferencing, pen pals, exchange visits, etc.)

Rashid (2000) reports an imaginative example of flexible educational support for a young black person in care which yielded many benefits.

> Mrs D considered that a family holiday to America, where members of the family welcomed Darren warmly, was significant in helping him to feel accepted. A second trip to America was planned when Darren was a teenager, but his school expressed concern about the impact of the absence on his poor attitude to his studies and his progress. The [foster] family's response was resourceful and imaginative. Mrs D contacted a black school teacher friend in New York who agreed to supervise work set by Darren's school in Britain. This proved successful and the teacher in New York helped Darren to modify some of his hostility toward school generally.
>
> *(Rashid, 2000, p.18)*

Examples of educational resilience

> One young woman, who had almost no opportunity to attend a mainstream school, and an appalling range of other adverse factors in her life, still finally achieved a good Honours degree from a leading English university. The only identifiable protective factors in her case were a passionate love of reading and an English teacher in a further education college who took a special interest in her.
>
> *(Jackson and Martin, 1998, p.578)*

> I am a 17-year-old girl, and I have been accommodated for four years, during which time I moved 22 times, across four regional divisions. As a result my schooling has been quite messed about . . . However, unlike a great many young people I returned to school. . . I had a particularly good relationship with one teacher. . . I was also very lucky to have incredibly strong support from the staff in the home who cajoled, conned and coerced me back into school. They kept telling me that I could succeed and made me believe it.
>
> *(Young woman in care who received encouragement from staff in the home to return to school, quoted in Sinclair, 1998, p.22)*

> They [foster carers] understood the education system. They worked with social workers but they knew a lot more, they knew the right steps to take and the right action. They made everything look like a challenge and made me attack it as a challenge and win. They pushed me through school and college.
>
> *(Norris, formerly in foster care and now a retail manager, quoted in Jackson and Martin, 1998, p.581)*

I hated the place, the big kids bullied you, they pinched everything you'd got and the teachers didn't care much about you at all, except Mrs. Johnson, she taught geography and made it interesting with videos and letters from kids abroad. I really liked it, you could talk to her about anything. She wasn't like a teacher at all. She seemed really pleased to see you when you came through the door.

(Boy who had experienced challenge of returning to old school from period in care, quoted in Bullock et al, 1993, p.182)

I remember once I had a very good school and I got on very well with the teachers there . . . I was there about a year and a half, and tension had built up inside me so much that I just had to talk to somebody and some perfectly trivial thing at school happened in a domestic science class. I can't remember what it was, and I started crying a bit, weeping, and the teacher was ever so sympathetic. She asked me to tell her all about it and when my tears had dried up a bit I went out and went home. It was the last period of school so I was OK. She must have spoken to the headmaster about it because soon after that a lot of the teachers assessed my work and I got a lot of individual attention from them, not to do with my own private affairs, but it made me feel as though, at last, I belonged to somebody or something or a group of society. I wasn't so cut off any more. I was very grateful to those teachers, especially the headmaster.

He arranged that I could take "O" levels and if it hadn't been for him I don't think I'd have had the courage to go into anything. I think I'd have been a very backward sort of person if it hadn't been for his egging me on to make something of myself, for myself. If my foster parents weren't interested I wasn't to worry. If nobody else was interested it didn't matter. He was interested, and I had to be for my own sake, for earning power and this sort of thing. It was really like a pep talk I got and he did quite a lot for me. I took some exams and passed them and it boosted my morale tremendously.

(Anne, quoted in Kahan, 1979, pp.159-160)

Carol, who grew up in residential care, wondered if this had influenced the way she was regarded.

The secondary school experiences were happy although she [Carol] felt the school was poor academically and that they were too lenient with her because she came from a home. She was very good at art and sport and was in nearly every sports team. She also made friends with a crowd which included a cousin of her future husband, an important chance link in her positive life-history.

(Quinton and Rutter, 1988, p.211)

Here are some examples of the importance of a teacher's mentoring relationship as a turning point.

A teenage girl living on a sink estate in a largish town had a father who was frequently in prison and a mother who was chemically dependent. She was doing poorly in school and seemed a likely candidate for early drop out. Out of the blue she made a positive connection with a new young English teacher. With her encouragement and support, the girl caught up and is now talking seriously (and realistically) about doing law in university.

(Source: personal communication with a workshop participant)

A workshop participant recalled how in his own school days, he had been getting a message in secondary school that he was unlikely to shine academically and should be planning his choice of subjects and career on that basis. When he was 14 or so, he recalls one young teacher taking him aside at the end of the year and saying more or less: 'Listen "boyo", don't heed this idea that you don't have ability. Work hard and you will do fine.' This man is now a successful manager in social services in an Australian city. Looking back, he regards that conversation and the encouragement of that teacher as a key turning point in his life.

(Source: testimony of a workshop participant)

Other adults in a young person's network can also play a supportive role in relation to education. This support may take the form of positive expectations, as in the example below.

A boy in long-term care had a strong friendship with another boy who was not in care. He spent a lot of time in this boy's house and grew quite close to the boy's mother. One day, the three of them were discussing the boys' future after they left school, and the woman said to the two boys 'when you both go to university. . .' The boy recalls this moment as a crucial boost to his confidence, that this woman, whom he trusted and respected, really believed that he would one day go to university. He did indeed go to university, is a graduate, has a good job, and is still in touch with his friend and the woman.

(Source: workshop participant)

A cautionary note

Beware the urge to encourage the young person to do well in school tipping over into pushing the young person too hard in order to satisfy adult ambitions. It is right for the young person to be challenged, but in a balanced way.

6 Promoting positive involvement in leisure activities

The experience of some form of success, accomplishment, or even just pleasure in activities may be important, not because it dilutes the impact of unpleasant or stressful happenings, but because it serves to enhance confidence and competence to deal with the hazards and dilemmas of life.

(Quinton and Rutter, 1988, p.197)

Why are activities important?

> The experience of some form of success, accomplishment, or even just pleasure in activities may be important, not because it dilutes the impact of unpleasant or stressful happenings, but because it serves to enhance confidence and competence to deal with the hazards and dilemmas of life.

(Quinton and Rutter, 1988, p.197)

There is a body of research evidence in support of the value of leisure-time activity for children experiencing adversity. Receiving strong positive recognition for an activity in which they engaged was found to be a protective factor for children living in disharmonious homes. For the purpose of this study:

> . . . recognition had to come from a source outside the family and included, for example, children who had won sports competitions, had paintings exhibited in a selective school exhibition, or had been chosen for a school football team.

(Jenkins and Smith, 1990, p.63)

In a study of African-American males in poor and violent neighbourhoods in the USA, skills and competence in certain activities were among the factors that the young men found helped them steer clear of violence.

> . . . music (particularly rap) was an important outlet and realm of competence. For other males, having a skill, for example, being good with computers, excelling in one or more academic subjects, being involved in a meaningful extracurricular activity or having mechanical ability, was a source of belonging, pride and self-esteem.

(Barker, 1998, p. 455)

Where young people may feel marginalised, as young people in care or in need sometimes do, leisure-time interests may help them to 'join or re-join the mainstream' (Smith and Carlson, 1997). Involvement in activities may reduce the risk of school drop out and may have most impact with students at high risk for drop out (Mahoney and Cairns, 1997). Participation in leisure activities may also be protective against the risk of behaviour problems (Borge, 1996). This seems to be especially the case where the activities are structured, engaged in voluntarily and 'are aimed toward skill building, rule guided, led by a competent adult, and follow a regular participation schedule' (Mahoney and Stattin, 2000, p.125). Mahoney (2000) reports that participation in extra-curricular activities with one's peer social network is associated with short-and longer-term positive outcomes. Such participants are less likely to drop out of school and/or to have been arrested as young adults.

Success and involvement in activities can prove a turning point in young people's lives, thus providing a pathway out of adversity. Bifulco and Moran (1998) recount the experience of one young sportswoman whose sport helped her escape an abusive home in the North of England and protected her from the risk of later mental health problems.

Triseliotis *et al* (1995) found that the young people in their study (who were clients of social services) were generally positive about involvement in activities and about the relationships with the befrienders or outreach workers who facilitated this involvement. Social workers also acknowledged the value of such involvement. In a few cases, 'the energies of youngsters with behaviour problems had apparently been successfully diverted into positive activities' (p.164). Both social workers and young people seemed to indicate that such activities, while beneficial, had generally not involved in-depth change or help.

Sample framework for assessing the demands and potential of different selected activities with reference to a given child

	Volleyball	Swimming	Horse riding	Tennis	Football
Low initial skill/aptitude level OK	✔	✔			
Low social interaction possible	✔	✔	✔		
Group activity essential	✔	✔			✔
Typically widely available	✔	✔			✔
Requires initial concentration for mastery	✔	✔	✔	✔	
Cost feasible	✔	✔			✔

Many young people [in residential care] have no significant interests, and greater emphasis needs to be placed on the importance of encouraging young people to have interests outside the residential unit, and to develop their social and recreational skills. The encouragement of these activities should be a specific part of the care plan for individual young people and children. Staff training should include the development of skills in this area.

(Skinner, 1992, p.49)

Arguing along similar lines, Sinclair and Gibbs conclude from their research on children's homes the need to recognise the value of opportunities for accomplishment for the residents.

The evidence supports the need to look at all aspects of a [children's home] resident's life, including school, leisure and work in order to encourage and support those things in which he/she can take a legitimate pride.

(Sinclair and Gibbs, 1998, p.156)

The potential value of foster carers gently introducing young people to spare time activities has also been acknowledged in a pioneering Kent family placement scheme.

> Foster parents were generally well informed about local activities, and their own children helped to integrate the newcomers. However, many adolescents in placement preferred individual pursuits, such as fishing or riding, to group activities . . . Foster care offered good opportunities for developing interests without too much pressure – for example, cooking, helping with decorating or other household jobs or caring for animals, and adolescents often learned to share their foster family's hobbies.
>
> *(Hazel, 1981, pp.116–7)*

Some of the issues surrounding spare time activities and youngsters in care are considered in the following sections. The discussion begins with the care of animals, and moves on to sport, cultural activities, and volunteering.

Caring for animals

The psycho-social significance of caring for and relating to animals

An animal may be warm, cuddly, responsive, loyal, non-judgemental, sensitive, reliable and constant. It can contain the secrets and stresses confided within it. This "listening ear" which an animal may provide may be very therapeutic for a child who finds it hard to access what he or she regards as a trustworthy human ear. The animal's behaviour, perceived by the child as reliable and responsive, may strengthen the child's sense of a secure base in the world. The animal can represent a comforting, precious and supportive constancy. It may signal very clearly its affection for the child, a child who may have been starved of such affection at many points in the past. The purring of a cat, the nuzzling by a horse, the wagging tail of a dog directed in recognition of a child familiar to the animal may prove healing gifts for the child craving acceptance and affection. This sense of "lovability" conveyed to the child by the animal may help to improve self-esteem.

> A quite disturbed boy placed with foster carers who were farmers was given a carefully monitored opportunity to hand-rear a baby lamb. This proved a very positive experience for the boy, whose behaviour and engagement with the carers improved. The dependence of the lamb and the trust it invested in the boy proved hugely therapeutic for him.
>
> *(Gilligan, 2000a, p.118)*

Over time the animal may invest trust in the child, an experience which the child may never have had either as the recipient or investor of trust in the past. The animal may come to depend on the care the child provides. The dependence of the animal confers a responsibility that the child may come to take very seriously. Discharging this responsibility may serve to enhance a child's self-esteem and self-efficacy. Care of the animal may introduce the child to a whole new set of peers, both young and old, who share a similar bond with this type of animal. This can be a valuable way of building a social network independent of the "in care" identity or status. Loyalty and commitment to the animal may earn the child not only the affection and trust of the animal but the admiration of adults who observe what is going on, thus further enhancing self-esteem. As the child gains further know-how and confidence in dealing with the animal, adults may seek advice or assistance from the young person. This might take the form of "baby sitting" animals or undertaking part-time or full-time work related to animals in, for example, a pet shop, kennels or stables.

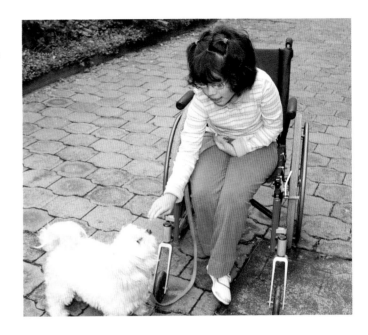

His latest activity is horse-riding. We often got complaints from school about how he could not sit still and concentrate for more than a brief moment. Miraculously, he can sit on a pony for over an hour and just move as necessary. It's incredible to see the concentration and work he can apply on horseback. The feeling of the big animal so close and the whole process of sitting and riding seems to work wonders at any age and for almost any child. He looks forward [to it] every week and is slowly but surely becoming more confident.

(Source: personal communication by foster carer of nine-year-old boy with learning difficulties)

The powerful meaning of relationships with animals for children in care means that they must be treated with great sensitivity. The death or departure of an animal must be recognised as the traumatic event it may be for the child. The death of a loved animal can be very hard for any child, even more so for the child in care for whom the lost bond with the animal may evoke echoes of other losses. Kate Cairns (2002) recalls the crisis when her foster daughter's ducks became seriously ill. They were the focus of her life and her closeness to them was an alternative to more contact with humans, many of whom had alienated the girl in earlier experiences. The vet was called and immediately sensed the emotional meaning for the girl of any possible loss. He handled the information about prognosis with great tact and sensitivity. He also applied great care and skill to the treatment as they all made a full recovery! But if the ducks had died it would have been a serious crisis, re-evoking past pain and losses unrelated to the ducks. But this does not mean that the risk of losing animals should be a bar to a child having the opportunity; as always, we need to apply wisely a risk-gain analysis.

The implications of any possible placement move, which may raise the spectre of separating child and animal, need to be considered very carefully. In such cases, placement planning must really strive to avoid any separation or rupturing of the relationship. It is often the animal that supplies the only meaningful constancy for the child in such circumstances. Social workers and carers may find themselves suddenly immersed in the care needs, not only of a child, but also of a dog or tropical fish.

Issues to be considered by carers and social workers in supporting a child's relationship with an animal

The following list is not to discourage the carer, nor the idea of the child having a companion animal. Indeed, the opposite is very much the intention. It is hoped that this discussion encourages greater appreciation of how much value children in care can derive from companion animals. But it is also hoped to highlight some of the issues that may inevitably arise and that need careful forethought.

- Adequate daily care of the animal (willingness of child's carer to take on final responsibility for the well-being of the animal as well as the child)

- Emotional significance of attachment to animal for child and implications of any rupture in relationship due to illness/death of animal

- Costs of feed/veterinary care

- Any implications posed by animal for relations with neighbours or neighbours' children

- Protection of animal from possible abuse or neglect due to disturbance/immaturity/ignorance of care needs on part of child or peers

- Long-term care arrangements in context of any placement moves

- Costs of special equipment (e.g. aquarium, kennel, hutch, etc)

- Transport of animal and its equipment

- Adequate briefing for young person's carers on animal's requirements

Whatever the challenges, the care of animals can greatly enrich children's lives.

Examples of animals offering opportunities for care/responsibility/interest

Horses/ponies
Baby lamb
Greyhound
Birds
Racing pigeons

Possible pets

Budgie
Cat
Dog
Hamster
Rabbit
Tortoise
Tropical fish

I used to go up to the horse about six o'clock, you know. The big red sun would be there, you know, and a beautiful day out . . . I'd go up and she would be knackered, you know, after she'd be running around with other horses all day and I'd go up to her and the second I'd touch her, she's gone, she's out for the count and I'd rub her and rub her and rub her and talk to her. It was a straightforward bond with that horse. It was like we had something going. If someone was annoying me I'd go up to the horse. I'd rather tell them than hurt anyone else. I'd tell me horse before I'd tell me old ma, you know what I mean? We used to sit down and I'd just rub her and rub her and she'd be just out for the count and the second I get up and leave she bounces back up again. I'd have to stay there until at least twelve o'clock at night until she's out for the count.

(Natalie Smith in Ogden, 1999)

Sport and other leisure pursuits

Sport offers many possible roles in the front line as a player, or in the background in preparation or around the "field of play". It may offer relatively safe risk taking for risk-seeking adolescents. It may offer a sense of belonging and a readymade set of peers and colleagues.

> My carers got me into karate. They got me all the stuff and came to watch me sometimes. You have to learn to control your temper when you're doing something like that, which I really needed at the time. I made some good pals up there too.

(Glenn, quoted in Happer et al, 2006, p. 35)

Horse care - examples of meaningful roles and activities for the interested young person

Feeding
Grooming
Instruction
Leading out beginners
Tending sick horses
Organising feed
Riding out
Slopping out stables
Preparation and transport for events
Tacking up (fitting bridle, bit, saddle, stirrups, etc)
Organisation of arena for instruction and training (see also Cooper, 1999)

Boys and girls with high levels of participation in sport may have a higher sense of self-worth than non-participants, as found in a large Northern Ireland survey (Trew, 1997). Sampling different sports can expose a young person to a variety of opportunities and roles that may help identify a latent talent or interest. It is also the case that not all sports require a high initial level of proficiency, social interaction or competitiveness. Swimming or fishing, for instance, may not demand a high degree of social interaction. Mountain, or more precisely hill, walking may not require a high degree of specific skill. Most sports can be played at an informal level. Particular sports can be introduced at a pace to suit the individual child. For a child lacking in confidence, it may be best to start gently with sporting activity more focused on undemanding individual performance and then move gradually to sport which requires more team work, social interaction or skill. There is evidence that teenagers may drop out of sport for a variety of reasons, a trend more marked among girls who may find the physicality and "public" nature of sport a challenge as they come to terms with the physical and psycho-social changes of adolescence. While recognising these trends, it is important that carers and concerned adults do not regard such tendencies as immutable facts. Many young people do continue an involvement, and with the right encouragement even more might do so.

Sport may literally help to change lives, as in these examples from Finland of a young man who had spent his teenage years in a reform school, and from Sweden of a young girl in foster care.

> [He] emphasised that being good at sports in adolescence changed his life. After being successful in boxing, he was offered an opportunity to join an army special group for athletics. This was good for his self-esteem. In his own words, being good at boxing was 'kind of like the first time I felt proud of something. I felt proud of myself'.
>
> *(Ronka et al, 2002, p. 55)*

> A young girl in foster care in Sweden joined her new foster family. The foster father and two sons were heavily involved in ice hockey, the father as team coach and the boys as players on the team. Very soon, with their encouragement and support, the girl became closely involved with the ice hockey team as the team mascot. She was fully decked out in the team supporters' regalia at every match. Her role as the team mascot helped her to join the family more fully. Not only did it help her to become more of a member of the family, it also helped her, presumably, to become integrated into the family's social network, thus also expanding, almost certainly, her own social network.
>
> *(Source: workshop participant, from Gilligan, 2008)*

Rowing offered several opportunities

Due to her skill at rowing, she was able to move to London and achieve a place in the national team, thus permanently changing her life for the better. Rowing not only represented an escape route from an abusive environment, it also opened up social and material opportunities she would otherwise never have had access to. Despite childhood neglect and abuse she developed a strong sense of purpose and good self-esteem which protected her against depression in later years.

(Bifulco and Moran, 1998, p.164)

EXAMPLES OF SPORTS OPEN TO YOUNG PEOPLE

Archery
Athletics
Badminton
Basketball
Boxing
Cricket
Cycling
Football
Gymnastics
Hockey
Horse riding
Netball
Olympic handball
Rowing
Sailing
Show-jumping
Skateboarding
Skiing
Squash
Swimming
Synchronised swimming
Table tennis
Ten pin bowling
Tennis
Volleyball
Weightlifting

Backroom activities in sport

Helping with:
Baggage and kit
First aid kit
Pitch marking/cleaning
Publicity
Equipment
Food and refreshments
Programmes/newsletters
Transport
Preparation of flags, bunting and mascots

At the match/event

First aid assistant
Photographer
Programme seller
Spectator
Supporter
Serving as team mascot
Water carrier
Video camera operator
Reporter for school newspaper
"Statistician" logging incidents

In competitive sport, the experience of success and failure can carry important psychological benefits. Success may raise self-esteem, and even failure may carry positive potential. The frustration of failure may prove cathartic for the young person in the associated release of frustration and hurt, which may well relate to arenas beyond those of sport. Coping with failure in the relatively benign and sheltered sphere of sport may also prove a valuable testing ground for coping with failure, when the stakes may be higher in "real life". The shared disappointment of defeated team members may forge a stronger bond of solidarity and support between the young person and team-mates and coaches. This may help the young person to develop precious social and perhaps even confiding relationships. It may also offer the young person valuable role models in terms of handling closeness and frustration in constructive ways.

Ten pin bowling

Eight years ago she joined a local ten pin bowling club . . . which caters for special needs children and young adults. She plays basketball with them every Saturday and ten pin bowling every Tuesday. She has been chosen to play on the Irish Bowling Team in the Special Olympics in Holland in May . . . I feel that her involvement in these sports has helped her in a very big way.

(Foster carer of 17-year-old-girl with mild learning disability who is in long-term foster care)

Taking up football

"John" joined a foster family consumed with football. Initially he joined in as a player but soon gave up, unable to cope with the rules and sanctions of the game. This was accepted, without fuss, by the foster family. Later in the placement he wanted to take up football again, this time coping well with the demands of the rules and of team play. Stable and positive foster care had nurtured a growing maturity.

(Case vignette from a workshop participant)

A number of objections arise fairly readily to a stress on the value of sport: firstly, not every child likes sport; secondly, not every child excels. Children who may lack confidence and emotional stability may be more liable to lack the physical co-ordination, motor skills, discipline and easy sociability so often necessary to do even passably well at sport. Emphasising sport may seem to be introducing one more potential area for failure and discouragement in the child's life. Thirdly, adults may have a philosophical reservation about the competitive nature of most sports and/or about the degree of violence and risk that may accompany some physical contact sports. Fourthly, there may be a view that a focus on sport tends to draw attention more towards boys, since there is evidence, as noted above, that as they get older many girls may veer away from active participation in sport, especially in team sports (Brooks and Magnusson, 2007).

It is important to take these points seriously. There should be no question of compulsion in relation to participation in sport. In the approach being promoted in this book, the emphasis is on tapping into children's interests, talents and strengths. In some cases, these qualities may be fairly evident. In other cases, experience and social conditioning may conspire to hide from view a child's potential. There is a case, therefore, for affording children the opportunity for "tasters" of different sports and social experiences to which they have not previously had access. But these tasters should not be forced down the child's throat and they should only lead on to further involvement if the child is clearly signalling a preference for this, or at the very least is not expressing resistance or protest, directly or indirectly. A period of "sticking with" an activity may be justified where there are no glaring objections, since it may take time for the child to take to the activity and for the requisite social confidence and modicum of skill to emerge. Very often an interest in an activity may only take proper root when friendships grow out of the shared activity and help to sustain the involvement.

On the question of not everyone excelling, it is important to remember that sporting activities and events involve a complex web of processes, relationships and events, many of which require a whole range of background supports so that the front-line performers can play their part. It is great if a youngster in care can "star" at the front-line, but many will not. But these others have the further possibility of benefiting from the myriad of background support roles that need to be played. Background roles also avoid many of the hazards of front-line contact and competition. But it should also be noted that seeking to insulate children from risk completely may be counter-productive, in that it may render them *less* able to cope when actually exposed to risk outside the gaze of protective adults. Sport, among other things, serves an important function in allowing children to learn, or rehearse, how to deal with risk, fear or threat in a real yet more structured and supportive way.

Taking up synchronised swimming

A girl placed in short-term foster care with her siblings was introduced to the sport of synchronised swimming by the foster carers who were devoted swimming enthusiasts. Long after her return to a materially deprived home, the social worker noticed the girl at the local swimming pool attending the same synchronised swimming club to which she had been introduced by the foster carers. This girl had literally taken something extra from her placement which she did not have beforehand.

(Gilligan, 2000a, p.117)

In relation to the issue of girls losing interest in sport, this may indeed be true. It should not, however, be regarded as immutable fact. There are complex reasons why some girls may lose interest. But it should not be assumed that all girls will not be interested. Nor should it be assumed that they cannot have their interest re-kindled, if this issue is approached in sensitive ways and in appropriate contexts. Remember that forms of physical exercise beyond sport may be attractive to girls, for example, dance.

It is also worth noting the fact that a boy or girl may change his or her mind about participating in a sport or activity. The main lesson is that he or she will take part if and when ready - the key is to leave the door open. It is not possible to force the pace or the interest.

A cautionary note

While adults may encourage and support young people in their sporting and leisure activity, it is important to realise that, at the end of the day, it is the young person who must decide if he or she is interested, as the following true story indicates.

A change in direction

A 16-year-old young woman in care had been an extremely good diver and had been tipped to represent her country in time. The problems associated with entering and living in care (including drug use) led her away from diving. At a later point, partly due to pressure from people she loved, she resumed training with her old coach, but it didn't work out. She had moved on and was a different person - she no longer had the ambition or motivation to pursue her previous commitment to the sport.

(Source: based on a personal communication from a social worker)

Removing barriers to participation

One teenage girl was a competent swimmer and a popular member of a local swimming club near her home. On entering public care she was placed over 50 miles from her home city in a children's home in a pleasant but remote rural village. The distances involved and the lack of comparable facilities nearby meant that she was deprived of continuing her involvement in swimming.

(Source: personal communication from colleague in social services)

Outdoor pursuits possibly open to young people

Abseiling
Camping
Canoeing
Diving
Fishing
Gardening
Hill walking
Horse riding
Mountaineering
Orienteering
Scouting
Scrambling
Trekking
Youth hostelling

Indoor pursuits possibly open to young people

Astronomy
Car/motor bike repair
Chess
Collecting stamps
Computers
Cooking
Dress design and dress making
Hair care
Needlecraft
Photography
Radio ham
Youth club

Could this question of preserving her swimming connection have ranked higher in care planning for this teenager?

Expressive/interpretative arts

The arts offer many forms of cultural expression and interpretation at many levels of competence and sophistication. There is a lot of scope for enjoyment at even the most informal and elementary levels. Getting involved may open up a whole range of possibilities previously closed off, as this young person in care illustrates.

> I always used to watch out the window at all the kids out playing and never go out and play with them. And it's just through perseverance and encouragement I got more confidence, but really the dancing had a lot to do with it. Being good at dancing was a real boost.
>
> (Jennifer, aged 18, quoted in Happer et al, 2006, p.35)

An awareness of the range of possibilities may alert adults to possible outlets for the talents and interests of young people.

Looking for inspiration?

To the busy carer or social worker, it may not always seem easy to find the right opportunity or outlet for the timid or sceptical youngster. Yet there may be many places to look for inspiration for other ideas for activities or pastimes. These may often be activities with connections to other parts of the child's life or social network.

- Interests or activities evident in the child's own personal history
- Interests or hobbies of carers
- Interests or hobbies of carers' older or adult children, or other relatives
- Interests or hobbies strong in the family background of the child
- Interests or hobbies strong in the ethnic or cultural background of the child (while not trapping the child within some cultural stereotype)
- Interests or activities strong in the culture and tradition of the area where the child now lives
- Interests or hobbies of social worker

Music

Brass instruments
Choir
Drums
Flute
Guitar
Individual singing
Joining a band
Karaoke sessions
Piano
Songwriting
Violin

Drama and other activities

Creative drama/
drama in education
Comedy shows
Juggling
Musicals
Plays

Dance

Ballet
Disco dancing
Hip-hop
Line dancing
Salsa
Traditional dancing

Crafts

Fabric painting
Making jewellery
Needlework
Papier maché
Pottery
Sculpture

Art

Computer graphics
Mural painting
Photography
Set designing
Sketching

Creative writing

Entering a creative
writing competition
Entries on MySpace
or YouTube
Keeping a blog
Keeping a diary
Sending letters to
friends
Writing for the
school magazine
Writing stories

Musicals – possible roles through which a young person may contribute and belong

Backstage crew
Chorus
Costume assistants
Costume creation
Front-of-house
team
Make-up assistants
Musicians
Performers
Poster design
Programme
production
Refreshments and
raffle
Scenery assistants
Scenery design
Ticket sellers

POINTS TO CONSIDER

Introducing a young person to an activity

When introducing a young person living in care to an activity group open to all comers, how much, if anything, should the carer/social worker say to the activity leader about the young person's care status?

What considerations might have to be weighed up in making such a judgement? What are the advantages and disadvantages of being forthcoming about the young person's care status?

Levels of engagement and support for which a young person may be ready

- The young person seems ready for individually tutored solo activity.

- The young person seems ready for group activity with selected peers.

- The young person seems ready for participation in an open group, where his or her involvement is sensitively shadowed.

- The young person seems ready for group activity in an open group where the leader has been briefed and is welcoming.

Joining the scouts

"Tony" came to live with a foster family who were deeply involved in scouting. He studiously avoided any interest in scouting for a long time, but about nine months into the placement, he suddenly announced that he might 'give this scouting business a bit of a go'. It has worked out so well that he now aspires to training as a scout leader.

(Case vignette from a workshop participant)

Playing to an audience

Her ability to play the recorder led to an invitation for a young girl in foster care to play before a church congregation. Her successful performance and the applause it earned had a distinct effect on the girl's confidence and self-esteem according to her foster carer. An occasion such as this would be an event in any child's life, but for this girl the sense of acceptance and accomplishment earned by the applause was particularly significant.

(Gilligan, 2000a, p.117)

Dancing

One youngster in care liked line dancing. It emerged an aunt also liked it and precious family contact for this isolated child in care was built around joint attendance with the aunt at line dancing.

(Source: example cited from the experience of a workshop participant)

A boy in care had his fees for dance school paid by the local authority because of his interest in dance as a hobby. He is now a professional dancer appearing in major dance shows.

(Source: example cited from the experience of a workshop participant)

One 15-year-old in foster care with a strong interest in music took up disco dancing three years ago. Last Christmas she performed as a dancer in the local town pantomime. She was then asked by the local village youth club to show some dances to the junior members and now she takes ten children for £1 per head for classes on a Saturday morning in a local hall. She has £5 for herself each week after paying £5 for the use of the hall.

(Source: personal communication by foster carer)

A girl in foster care had a talent for drawing and illustration which had her in regular demand for the design of posters, covers for newsletters and so on in the local community. In the view of her foster carer, this talent had a great value in building her social confidence and self-esteem.

(Gilligan, 2000a, p.118)

A boy in care had developed a great love and knowledge of birds, partly because he lived in an area famed for its wildlife. The boy also had a great ability for drawing local birds. His school arranged for his work to be promoted through an exhibition and in local publications. But the most precious gain from his talent was an eventual and very rare acknowledgement of his ability from his normally indifferent mother.

(Source: workshop participant)

Volunteering

For a child who has been cast in a dependent and passive role for most of his or her life, the opportunity to be cast in the role of giver rather than recipient may have special meaning and significance. To be trusted by the recipient or the organiser of the service may be very affirming for the young person. To do something which is valued may not be a familiar experience for the young person. Volunteering may allow the child to gain not only confidence and self-esteem, but also skills and contacts. It may give the young person the chance to exercise responsibility and be trusted by others. Both such opportunities are likely to offer considerable developmental and therapeutic value. Voluntary experience may rate highly with an employer weighing up the merits of competing applicants. The voluntary work may itself lead directly to some work opportunities.

> As part of school-sponsored work experience, a boy in care was given the opportunity to help out with gardening and other tasks in a local nursing home. He was a boy who lacked confidence socially, but in the nursing home he proved to be a huge hit and enjoyed himself thoroughly. After the school-linked commitment was over, he wanted to keep up his involvement, and has organised a weekly commitment as a volunteer. The whole experience has been hugely positive for his development.

(Source: workshop participant)

This example illustrates how such voluntary or leisure time experience may offer a young person the opportunity to re-invent themselves, often adapting positively to the favourable expectations and responses of well-intentioned adults. But in some cases, young people may initially lack the confidence or grace to carry off front-line personal service to the public or people in need. But they may be able to help build or paint the floats for a community parade or help in a mail-out for an environmental campaign, or do a mail drop on a housing estate to publicise a community cause or event. They may have the technical know-how to assist in a hospital radio station or to make the internet accessible to the less initiated.

Karen Wilkins

If he or she has the confidence (and materials) required, then a youngster in care may enjoy offering free face-painting at community events and the plaudits and appreciation they earn from satisfied children and their parents. There is no reason why their in-care status should figure in the process – they are merely acting as young community members who wish to contribute something to the community. If they are good with a camera, they may like to take photographs of community events or at parties. They may be able to have these included in community magazines or newsletters; getting their name credited by the photograph may be a source of satisfaction and do their sense of self-esteem and self-efficacy a lot of good.

> A teenage boy in care who was doing well in school had the opportunity to go on a school exchange trip to Portugal. When the school checked with social services, the teachers were told that sanction for the boy travelling would only be given if a satisfactory child protection check could be done on the Portugese host family household where the boy was due to stay. The boy was deeply embarrassed at such a prospect and wanted to abandon any notion of travelling with his classmates.

(Source: conference participant)

POINTS TO CONSIDER

Given that any reasonable observer would think that such a trip would be good for this boy, how can our social services respond more like the "prudent parent" they undoubtedly aspire to be, rather than appear almost as a remnant of some totalitarian bureaucracy, with policies which, ironically, a child may actually experience as abusive or oppressive?

Dealing with typical objections to supporting participation in informal educational/sporting activities

Some possible objections one can imagine:

> It is wrong to pamper these children, they won't have these opportunities when they go home.

(Local authority member)

> My children don't have these opportunities.

(Unimpressed administrator)

> Giving children such opportunities puts their parents in a poor light.

(Sceptical social worker)

> It would make more sense to invest any such expenditure in counselling or therapy for these children.

(Sceptical carer)

He has tried lots of things but sticks at nothing. It's a waste of time and money to try anything else.

(Another sceptical carer)

She doesn't have the social skills to get on with people at any of these activities.

(Yet another sceptical carer)

Everything you suggest, she just turns up her nose at.

(Frustrated carer)

If kids have the capacity to get involved and stick at activities, then they don't really have problems in the first place.

(Another sceptical social worker)

The idea behind giving children in care such opportunities is not to use them as "treats" or "goodies" to pamper them. Nor is it to use them in some shallow attempt at compensating them materially for earlier or enduring emotional deprivation. Such activities – if the right one can be found for the particular child's interests and aptitudes – serve to give the child a medium within which they can explore more facets of themselves and their relationships with others. They may also help the young person to discover new competencies that may enhance self-esteem and self-efficacy, and build social relationships and contacts that may enhance their sense of a secure base and social support in the world. Ideally, they will acquire a leisure-time interest and capacity which they can carry with them into the adult world and also a set of social relationships which takes them well beyond the ghetto of the care system, as the following example shows.

From the start, S. [my foster mother] would bring me up to the tennis courts, sometimes with a school friend, and we would play simple tennis games until I got the hang of the skills. For many years the local tennis club provided a social as well as a sporting environment for me – I befriended many people, some my own age, some a good deal older – whom I still keep in touch with. I also went on to coach in the Kit Kat Dublin Tennis League for a few years as well as coaching in a camp in the US for the summer.

(Source: personal communication from a 22-year-old contented graduate of foster care)

7 The role of adults – carers, mentors, social workers, agencies

Frank used to, when he used to come home, he used to make sure he had loads of time to spend with you. He used to help us fix our pushbikes and then when we got older he used to help us. And he used to take us down to the docks all the time and I used to get to know people he worked with . . . He wasn't one of these people who say, oh, bugger off and watch telly. If you got your scalextric out or playing cards or whatever – he'd always find time. Even if it was, 'Half hour and I'll be with you'. . . but he always used to find time.

(Luke, speaking about his foster father, quoted in Schofield, 2003, pp. 46-7)

Giving time to the young person

The adults who work with and look after the young person in care need to offer care, patience and hope. In a real sense their task is to keep alive the possibility that things can get better, that positive change can happen, even when this prospect looks least likely. The adults involved may need to remember that the difficulties along the way – before and during life in care – may mean that the young person may take longer to get to a certain point of maturity or development than it may take a young person who has not had such pressure in their lives. It is important not to over-react when things go wrong and not to assume that things have gone permanently wrong even if there are some serious glitches along the way.

> Real parents would try to help, even if you were older, and young people who have been in care might need more time than others to work things out and get themselves settled down. They need to kick back a bit – they shouldn't be punished for it forever.
>
> (Carrie, quoted in Happer et al, 2006, p. 52)

In a sense, it might be said that the crux of working with young people in care or in need is to give them *time*. This idea of "giving time" needs to be understood in two senses – one most relevant at the level of personal care, and the other most relevant at the level of policy:

- *giving time* – in the sense of an adult giving one's own personal interest and attention. This is particularly important in the case of those adults who are quite closely involved in the young person's life, and ideally involves at least one adult who will have a long-term engagement with the young person.

- *giving time* – in another sense, this time, in terms of allowing young people more time in which to come good, to find their way, to get on track. Because young care-leavers may encounter serious problems at the time of leaving care or in the early years thereafter, we should not assume that that is the end of the story. Time may bring some recovery and some improvement. The difficulties these young people encounter along the way may just mean that their progress is delayed, but that eventually they will get there or to a good part of the way – it will just take them more time. It may be that for some, at least, the price of time in care and its accompanying stressors is not failed development but slower development.

In a sense, this gives a new orientation to service provision for young care-leavers. While a basic safety net of support is clearly critical, the primary aim of services might usefully be focused on finding *time* for the young person – in the senses used above. The role of the service is not primarily to give such time but rather to do two important things. Firstly, their role should be to identify and support the potential or actual "givers" of time, and secondly, their role should be to give hope, to instil a sense that things can and will get better, given *time*. Linked to this is the importance of not getting in the way, of not obstructing opportunities that may actually be building blocks to progress. One such example might be learning to read, or being motivated to learn to read, as a possible first step to a training course at a later point.

Time may heal

It is important not to give up hope when things seem to go wrong, when all the efforts adults have made seem to be coming to nought as the young person decides at a critical moment to "do their own thing". The following scenarios illustrate what can happen.

Recognising the possibility of progress

Some staff from a leaving care team were devastated that a young person in whom they had invested huge effort and whom they saw as having a very bright future decided, against all advice, at 18 to return to live in an extremely troubled family home. The young woman had been in care for very good reasons. The staff members of the project were very gloomy about her prospects at the point I met them. Just then, and understandably, they found it hard to take a positive and long-term view looking back and looking forward. I tried to reassure them that the positive investment that had been made in the young woman by all the caring adults in her life to this point would almost certainly pay dividends eventually. One or two wobbles along the way did not necessarily mean that everything had come undone. But in the middle of an apparent crisis, this was not easy to see. The important thing was not to lose faith in the possibility of positive progress. But, in that case, it was possible that it might take some time and some experimental assertion of her own identity and autonomy, before the young woman might come on track in terms of realising her potential. This may not happen quickly but in such situations it often does come right if the adults can give the situation and the young person time.

A good ending . . . eventually

A very troubled girl proved especially difficult for her foster carers in her placement. Yet they also recall her positively as being very memorable and appealing in many ways. Eventually, she ran away with a boy who had his own difficulties and this led on to her engaging in prostitution and becoming addicted to crack cocaine in a real drug/crime blackspot of a major city. Her foster carers were very upset at all of this and spent a great deal of time thinking of her. They were very gloomy about her future, assuming that she was on the road to an early death, if not already dead. A long time passed and there was no word. But one day they got a call from her out of the blue. She said she had always remembered them and how much

she got from them, even if she didn't show it at the time. She had been befriended by a Salvation Army officer who had helped her in her rehabilitation. She was now getting married to a worker in a Christian agency. She said she would have liked her foster father to give her away, but she had very recently become reconciled in her relationship with her birth father and she felt she had to ask him first.

(Source: workshop participant)

Carers and parents

It is often the little things that carers do that register with and reassure children. It seems that, through these little things, the carers somehow communicate interest and concern and help the child feel connected to the carer. At times, carers are also remembered for how they could also tune into the world of children. Anne recalls liking "Dad" Todd, a house-father who, with his wife, ran her residential unit for a time.

"Dad" Todd used to take us for walks, it was like going for a walk with a big brother. He was super, and one of the best things was, he used to muck about. If you wanted to sit and catch tadpoles, he would sit on the wall, kicking his legs and watch us, and join in the fun. I used to think that was great and when we were actually walking, we would go for miles with him, we'd be tearing about all over the road and everywhere, and I remember I used to hang close, you know, if I got the slightest chance I was holding his hand. I can remember that, and if anybody else got his hand I was madly jealous, He was very friendly in that way and I felt it was all right, I had a friend, not necessarily someone I could tell my troubles to, just a person in the background, like a big teddy, to run to for comfort.

(Anne, at the age of 20, recalling a part of her life in care, quoted in Kahan, 1979, p. 71)

There is a good deal of anxiety today around the role of men as carers, especially as foster carers. What tends to get lost is the potential of what men have to offer as carers (Gilligan, 2000c), something which Anne's account above emphasises.

It is also clear from children's accounts that the care they experience often comes from people who do not have a formal role as "carer" in their lives. Andrew recalls the importance of a relationship he developed with a cook in a residential unit.

She [the cook] always seemed ever so interested in what I did and she always treated me as someone special. Whenever there were roast potatoes, she knew that I liked roast potatoes and she would always make a point of saving a couple for me, and as soon as meals were finished I would creep into the kitchen and she would say, 'I've got you roast potatoes on a plate in the larder,' and I used to creep inside and hide in the larder eating those roast potatoes. I really felt towards that woman, she was there every day, she was part of our life.

(Andrew, at the age of 34, quoted in Kahan, 1979, pp. 71-2)

While we might be slightly uncomfortable from today's vantage point about favouritism towards one at the expense of the group, there is no doubt that partisan commitment is a hallmark of deep caring. It is very affirming to be on the receiving end of partisan caring, especially for a young person who may have known hard times inside and outside the care system. It may feel like a very warm place to have such attention and commitment. It is also worth noting that the impact of a carer is not necessarily related to the length of contact. Relatively short relationships – but which really connect – may be remembered for a long time afterwards. It may be consoling or daunting for carers to realise that they may have an impact which could last well into the future even when they have relatively short contact with a child in their care. The kind words we use, the encouragement we give, the warm memories we leave, the interests we inspire are each rich legacies that the young person may tap into and recall appreciatively many times later in life. Even simple kindnesses may resonate down the years and may serve as important modelling for the young person when they, in turn, take on caring roles and look for caring "scripts" in their memory bank.

> When I first met Trish I was stroppy and depressed. I was very low in confidence, in loads of debt, and my only income was Jobseeker's Allowance. I would sit in my flat all day with my life slowly going nowhere. Trish actually helped. She became someone I could talk to and someone I could trust. She soon became my best friend.
>
> Gradually, Trish started to take me out, all the time making me believe in myself and that life outside my little flat wasn't so bad. I think Trish has got a real passion for what she does; I didn't ever think that anyone would care so much about my life and where I was heading. She is always there when I need her, I can phone her anytime.
>
> My confidence has returned, I am not in debt anymore. And I have a job which I love. I'm in this position simply because someone liked me for who I am. Someone made me believe in myself and didn't give up on me when I had a strop.
>
> *(Young person, nominating her leaving care worker for the Believe in Me Awards 2007, organised by the Who Cares? Trust, quoted in Bond, 2008, p. 18)*

And other adults who have a less direct caring role may still be very important in the influence they exert and the messages they give the young person. They may help to inspire interests and encourage talents.

> My aunt would always say, 'Why don't you be a writer?' 'Cause I would always write her poems. She loved poetry. 'Write me another poem.' She would

always do that . . . So I would sit there and write things for her. She loved that. She's like, 'Gosh, you know you should be a writer.' And so that would motivate me, and so, of course, I kept writing things.

(Quoted in Hines et al, 2005, p.389)

A young woman asylum-seeker from the Democratic Republic of Congo had this to say about her key worker.

My key worker I could talk to about everything really. My key worker and some of the others – they always used to be there for me. They always used to come and talk to you and help you express your feelings. It was comfort really so it made me feel comfortable to talk to them about everything. I was feeling sad, I was feeling lonely that I was away from my family so they really helped.

(Quoted in Chase et al, 2008, p. 73)

The following example concerns a young boy, John, in a residential unit who loved nothing more than to spend time in the kitchen helping to bake cakes. He had interest and ability, and also thrived in the one-to-one attention involved in baking with the particular care worker. John was not a star at school and still struggled to read. But as he got more interested in baking and cookery he saw that his mentor used cookery books a lot and he soon wanted to be able to read the recipes so that he too could deliver successful results. With this stimulus, John quickly became a more motivated student and a more proficient reader.

(Gilligan, 2007, p.97)

The positive things carers can offer young people may stretch well beyond the period when they are officially recognised as carers, as these two examples illustrate. The symbolic and practical messages given by different adults at crucial moments in a young person's life may have long-term meaning. These messages may open up or close down possibilities. One powerful example is a young woman who grew up in care in an arrangement that had the blessing of her birth parents and the commitment of her foster carers. On the day of her wedding, she was walked down the aisle by both her own father and her foster father. In this other example, it becomes clear how a former foster home may become a haven in later life. A young man who had spent time in foster care is now in the armed forces and is frequently sent abroad with his unit, often to war zones. His former foster carers still play a very important part in his life. He spends his terms of leave with them. They offer a most precious haven in his adult life.

Adoptive parents can play a similar role, and often an enhanced one, because of the permanence they can offer.

I was 19 before I really experienced my first dose of overt racism. The word "nigger" was barked in my face by a Teddy Boy who I'd been staring at in admiration. It took me a while to realise who he was talking about. A few months later, someone suggested hailing a cab for me because that's the only way I'd get one. The person was white and was amazed that it hadn't occurred to me before.

Things then began to escalate . . . Throughout this necessary and turbulent period it was the indomitable and consistently deep love of my parents and family that encouraged me to work through it. That's what gave me my sense of self and the subsequent strength and confidence to cope. Love gives you the impetus to find your own identity, regardless of colour. It also equips you to deal with the universal pain of prejudice and rejection, as much as anyone can be equipped to deal with it.

(Clare Gorham, quoted in Harris (ed), 2006, pp. 302-3)

Mentors

Mentoring - a suggested definition

Adults who have a positive influence in a young person's development, consciously or unconsciously, may be playing a mentoring role. There is considerable interest in the idea of mentoring as a way of supporting vulnerable youngsters. The idea of mentoring may also be helpful in work with young people in care. The term "mentoring" can be used in a number of senses: a possible definition of the role is offered here.

Mentoring uses a relationship for the purposeful encouragement of a (young) person's all round development or that of some facet of their competence. It is likely to work best as a relationship when based on a shared enthusiasm for some common activity. Mentoring thus involves an element of reciprocity in that the encouragement and guidance of the adult are rewarded by the absorption of the youngster into a higher state of competence and commitment.

The mentoring relationship thrives on a shared interest and the enjoyment of time spent together. In a US study of adolescent mothers, the researchers noted the importance of mentors in the progress of those who had done well: 'While the low achievers rarely spoke of having mentors, *all* [emphasis in original] of the high achievers spoke of having at least one person in their lives who was supportive and encouraging of their educational and occupational endeavours' (Way and Leadbetter, 1999). Typically, outside of family, mentors spoken of included 'godfathers, aunts, babysitters, older women, friends and teachers.' An Australian study on the fate of care-leavers observed the significance of a mentoring type relationship in the progress of the young people: 'Often having someone to take an interest in their sporting or other activities helps to sustain their interest in positive community activities and avoids them becoming isolated' (Maunders *et al*, 1999).

A close relationship with an adult outside the home was found to buffer children from the effects of living in a disharmonious home (Jenkins and Smith, 1990). In this study the adult was almost always a grandparent although other people may also play this supportive role. The power of helpful adults is confirmed in other research.

> Our own research, as well as that of our American and European colleagues who have followed resilient children into adulthood, has repeatedly shown that, if a parent is incapacitated or unavailable, other persons in a youngster's life can play such an enabling role, whether they are grandparents, older siblings, caring neighbours, family day care providers, teachers, ministers, youth workers, big brothers and big sisters, or elderly mentors.
>
> *(Werner and Smith, 1992, p. 208)*

Triseliotis *et al* (1995) found that some of the young people in care or receiving help in their study had access to a volunteer or paid befriender or outreach worker:

> A befriender is an adult who takes a special interest in a young person, normally engaging them in enjoyable activities to gain co-operation and trust . . . befriending seemed to be available largely on an *ad hoc* basis . . . Normally, the contacts had involved out-of-home activities like swimming, fishing, pool, ice-skating, canoeing and hiking. These were provided both to compensate for limited opportunities at home and as a means of gaining the youth's trust.
>
> *(p. 105)*

There may be a reasonably strong case for including mentors or befrienders in the repertoire of responses that might be included in customised packages of care for young people. Triseliotis *et al* (1995, p. 164) found, however, a number of barriers which blocked such an option: agency policy precluding such a possibility where the child had family contact; social workers being unaware of such a possibility; a shortage of the necessary personnel or resources; and agency resistance based on the notion that the relevant needs were already being served by professionals, or because the befriender was seen as a recycled version of the now outmoded voluntary visitor to children in care.

Finding a mentor

Who might be a potential mentor in the life of a child in care (other than a carer)? While mentoring schemes which recruit mentors and match them to young people are currently fashionable, it seems even more desirable that the mentor is someone whom the young person already knows and trusts, or at least is well known to someone whom the young person knows and trusts. In this way, ideally, the young person may go on to have a long-term connection with the adult concerned, something much less likely in "engineered" mentoring. Finding a ready-made and willing "organic" mentor in the natural network of the young person of course may not always be possible.

Serendipity, on the other hand, may also play a part in helping to find quite unexpectedly an influential adult. The following example illustrates this point with the story of a man who clearly played a key mentoring role in the young person's life, in this case, a young man sent to juvenile prison in the US who here recalls later in life the importance of the relationship and the value of their shared interest.

> He loved amateur radio. And he got me interested in radio and electrical stuff and things of that nature . . . He saw the potentials in me. He saw I enjoyed electricity. I enjoyed radio and stuff like that. He took me under his wing. And I thought an awful lot of this guy in a short ten months I worked with him. He was a prince . . . I prepared my whole life in ten months to do something. Think about it. Those ten months were crucial in my life. Because they turned me around. [Name of prison] turned me around. Jack turned me around. Jack was a humanitarian and cared for me as an individual. Let's get down to brass tacks. What if Jack wasn't there? What if I wasn't offered the opportunity? . . . He treated me right. As a matter of fact, after I left [name of prison] year after year on a yearly basis I would take my wife and kids, we'd drive all the way to [name of prison] to see Jack.

('Gilbert' in Laub and Sampson, 2003, p. 141)

Possible sources of mentors

Family friend
Friend/connection of carer
Friend/connection of social worker
Member of local faith community
Member of local community
Member of relevant special interest group
Neighbour
Relative
School contact
Someone specially recruited
Workplace

Possible sources of mentors

Either way, whatever the origins of the mentor, it is important that the person undertaking the mentoring role and relationship is "clued in" to certain "ground rules" about the relationship. How this is done may require sensitivity and tact, especially for those people offering their involvement quite informally from within the child's natural social network. In assessing the suitability of a given person as mentor, the young person's attitude should be a fairly important guide. Where the young person feels at ease and comfortable with the mentoring figure this may serve as a possible initial indicator. Where a potential mentor is less well known to the young person or their carer, certain key questions may need to be considered.

While one would not wish to trap young people who formerly were in care within the care system or have them feel that they have some extra obligation, it is the case that young people who have moved on and made their way in the wider world may have something to offer to young people still in care and may wish to have the opportunity to do so.

POINTS TO CONSIDER

Assessing a potential mentor	Yes	No
Has technique/skill and enthusiasm to share with youngster	❏	❏
Is known to adults committed to the child	❏	❏
Has experience of relating to children	❏	❏
Has been vetted for child protection if not already well known	❏	❏
Knows where to bring issues of child protection or issues of similar complexity	❏	❏
Has received notes of guidance and had opportunity to discuss same	❏	❏
Understands meaning of relationship to child and consequent need for reliability	❏	❏
Appears not to "need" the relationship with the child	❏	❏
Is willing to liaise as necessary with the child's carer or social worker, or with an appropriate key adult in the child's social network	❏	❏

Creating opportunities

How can agencies placing children ensure that carers are alert to the value of activities and the opportunities for such that exist in their local communities?

What might act as barriers to young people participating and how might these be removed?

Should agencies introduce incentives (e.g. more pocket money) for young people in care to encourage and give recognition for achievements in school or wherever – an idea floated by a young black woman formerly in care? (Dickson, 1995, p.160)

In what ways might agencies create opportunities not otherwise available to young people in care to broaden their horizons and promote opportunities for self-development and self-expression?

Social worker

The social worker has the challenging task of holding together the whole picture of the young person's life, across the past, the present and the future – and across the different arenas that are important to the young person. While the emphasis necessarily must be on the social supports and challenges evident in each area of the young person's life, many would wish to emphasise how important it is that social workers and others pay attention to educational progress particularly.

> Most social workers don't seem to have education as a focus. They need training to make them think more carefully about who goes where, who they'll be living with, will they share, will their foster carers support them with studying and appreciate that they want to do well at school and college.
>
> *(16-year-old in foster care, quoted in Harker et al, 2003, p. 97)*

What qualities in their social worker are valued by young people who are in care or who are clients of the child welfare system more generally? Triseliotis *et al* (1995, p. 272) found in their study that adolescent clients got on well with helping adults who:

- were informal in approach (e.g. were easy to talk to or took the young person out);

- respected young people, listened to what they said, tried to understand and did not lecture them;

- could recognise the difference between being frank and sometimes challenging from being "pushy" and "nagging";

- were available, punctual and reliable;

- did practical things to help;

- carried out their promises.

The social worker's relationship with the child's carers is also an important influence on the course of things. Thoburn *et al* (1998, pp.38–9) identified a number of important considerations based on their study of 297 minority ethnic children in adoptive or permanent foster homes. From their observations, they consider it helpful for the social worker to serve as a "sounding board". The key seems to be to help carers to find their own context-and culturally-appropriate answers rather than having these prescribed from outside by the social worker. The social worker can help – but on the family's terms as much as possible. In a memorable phrase, the authors stress that the social worker should resist the temptation to "back seat drive" in the placement. The trick also is to use low-key opportunities to discuss issues, such as on the occasion of annual picnics or whatever. This allows matters to be treated as "no big deal", to use the author's insightful term.

From their research, Triseliotis *et al* (2000) relate what the carers in their study would like to teach social workers to do:

- 'be more available, more supportive and reliable;
- be better listeners;
- work more in partnership;
- understand what hard work fostering is;
- provide honest information about the children and their background;
- use more common sense;
- think of the carers' family;
- learn more about children; and
- sometimes act as foster carers.'

(pp.150–1)

While social workers must support the carers, in a different capacity they must also work in the interests of the child in placement. It may be helpful to think of the social worker as a mediator in the matrix of relationships which embrace and constitute the complexity of the "case" which represents a child's life in care.

> The social worker's role might be better constructed as "mediator" rather than "authority", with emphasis being placed on the need for detailed attention to the voice of all those centrally involved in thinking about the child's needs and future placement possibilities and on the need for negotiation between the potentially conflicting views of these participants.
>
> *(Cooper and Webb, 1999, p. 133)*

Another role for the social worker in work with children in care may be that of negotiator, especially where the young client opposes the former's decisions and duties.

Social service agencies

While the social worker plays a key role in the lives of children in care (Gilligan, 2000d), it is clear that the policies and procedures of agencies bear heavily on the social worker's approach and the child's experience.

Challenges for practice and policy

This book offers many ideas for a more optimistic and child-centred practice. Yet the ideas all suppose many challenges for practice which need careful thought and attention.

- How to give sufficient emphasis to the crucial task of assessment.

- How to 'have a life course perspective and not the short-term perspective often found in social work practice' (Andersson, 1999).

- How to identify the talents and interests of young people in care.

- How to preserve quality friendships of young people in care in the face of placement moves.

- How to deal with the young person's surface response of "not interested" or "this is boring".

- How to deal imaginatively and *proportionately* with the child protection issues which can arise in pursuit of hobbies and extra-curricular activities, ensuring the potential significant benefits of these are included in any balanced risk-gain assessment.

- How to deal with the resource requirements (equipment, travel, insurance, costs, etc.).

- How to find the time that well paced encouragement and preparation may require.

- How to sequence exposure to activities so that less challenging/socially threatening activities come first.

- How to promote vital qualitative research to deepen our understanding of the specific interplay of risks, personal qualities/experiences and environmental factors which promote a resilient response to adversity in a given individual (Fraser *et al,* 1999).

What agencies can do to promote resilience- and strengths-led approaches

While the complexity of providing well for children in care should not be underestimated, there are various steps which may help to improve the care that individual children receive.

- Prepare an attractive agency handbook aimed at young people, carers and social workers outlining information about options and contacts for activities.

- Declare a commitment to promoting opportunities to participate in informal educational activities.

- Establish a scheme of subsidies and supports – for activities and equipment.

- Ensure access to quality after-school programmes for young people in care. Research suggests that such schemes may be of particular benefit to vulnerable young people (Posner and Vandell, 1999).

- Have available an annual budget for each young person in care to spend on such activities.

- Engage in partnership schemes with relevant outdoor pursuit, sporting and cultural organisations.

- Ensure a child protection policy which is truly child centred and which balances notions of safety with notions of welfare and developmental opportunity.

- Develop links with local business and opinion leaders with a view to generating ideas, goodwill, useful contacts, fundraising and so on. Such people are likely to be very attracted by a scheme which aims to assist young people to build confidence and competence and does so on terms which these local leaders can understand. The right combination of business people, lawyers, judges, educationalists, media people and community leaders could be a very helpful resource in terms of accessing support and opening doors when necessary. It could also help spread more positive understanding about the needs, problems and potential of young people in the care system.

- Explore the possibility of appointing an artist-in-residence to a children's home or comparable residential unit, or to the social services local office to serve local foster children. (Such an appointment might be funded from an arts rather than a social services budget.)

- Be willing to take risks in the interests of the longer-term development and well-being of the young person (see the example of the horse lover whose interest was encouraged, in Schofield and Brown, 1999).

- Ensure that young people in care are not deprived of opportunities to participate in activities available to their peers because of lack of interest or initiative by their carers.

> With regard to recreational activities, respondents listed a rich variety of activities that they did in their spare time, both in the home and outside, most of them mentioning several. When asked if there was anything else they would like to do, some gave quite imaginative answers, with bungee jumping getting several mentions, along with the prospect of meeting the Arsenal football team! However, more often the chosen activities were more easily achievable, such as going to Brownies, swimming and after school clubs. The wish list for some children was almost exactly the same as the list of what other young people were doing, suggesting that this is an important area to ask about since some carers will not be as active as others in providing these social opportunities.
>
> *(Baldry and Kemmis, 1998, pp.36-7)*

8 The young person linking into the wider world

And someone like Pete [social worker] has been a great inspiration to me . . . because he's been a caring character . . . I'm not saying he's like a father figure all the time, but I know he's there . . . [After prison] I decided I didn't want to get my hands dirty anymore and I wanted to be driving a nice car . . . rather than working on it and decided to do an Access to Higher Education course for over 21s and spent a year doing that . . . by the time that happened . . . I applied for a place at university and it all went from there . . . And it still ain't sunk in yet.

(Barry, who grew up in foster care, quoted in Schofield, 2003, p. 196)

The challenge of entering the adult world

> I joined the army in January and I've done my training and just passed out. I've got loads of qualifications and met lots of good mates. It's amazing. A big achievement because I never thought I would make it. I've done it and I pleased everybody and it's a great feeling.
>
> *(Mark quoted in Happer et al, 2006, p.39)*

A number of factors are likely to have helped Mark succeed in "passing out" in the army. The structure and discipline of the military, his own ambition and agency, the support and expectations of carers or family, the new friends he had made. The quote from Mark illustrates well the mix of ingredients that may help a young person to make positive progress as they begin to make their way in the world.

It seems likely that, as Mark's story implies, social support may be a very important ingredient in terms of assisting a young person to do better when they leave care. Four points seem relevant here. Firstly, it is important that such support is genuinely available and in forms relevant to the young person's needs. Secondly, it is important that the young person feels able to avail themselves of such support, that they are actually comfortable asking for help. Thirdly, the most important dimension of support for the young person may be their sense that support actually exists and is ready to be called upon. Fourthly, the reality that young care leavers are facing up to these issues with less support and time to adjust than their more privileged peers makes the issue of support crucial.

> I've been living with Sylvia and John for about three-and-a-half years. I've been through a lot in my life. I come from Macedonia and lost my family in the war – but living with John and Sylvia makes me feel at home. They are always there for me when I need them. I don't feel left out, because they take good care of us – like one of their own. The word "foster" to me is just a word. We are a family. We all look after each other. This lovely couple are the best English people I have ever met. They are always there to talk to.
>
> *(Arber, 18, nominating his foster carers, Sylvia and John Denning, for the Believe in Me Awards 2005, organised by the Who Cares? Trust, quoted in Bond, 2008, p.15)*

For young care-leavers, three sources of such support seem particularly important depending on individual circumstances: parents, former carers and siblings. Indeed, older siblings may play a 'quasi-parental role, providing advice, guidance and practical support' to care leavers (Wade, 2008):

> I think [his sister] helps him feel like he's got a home, even though he doesn't live there. He can go and get his washing done there and she's very caring and accepting of him.
>
> *(Leaving care worker quoted in Wade, 2008, p. 45)*

The most valuable place to start when trying to put support in place is building on familiar connections the young person already has. This may help to make it a little easier to ask for help and a little more likely that they will get the kind of help when they need it. Generally a person who knows the young person is more likely to have the commitment to be responsive in a way that makes a difference and in a spirit that makes it easier for the young person.

For many young people who have grown up in care, it may be important to have a sense of back-up when they enter into the "real world" of work with all its demands. A young man who had spent time in foster care is now in the armed forces and is frequently sent abroad with his unit, often to war zones. His former foster carers still play a very important part in his life. He spends his terms of leave with them. They offer a most precious and sympathetic haven of peace in his adult work life.

For young women who have been in care and who become pregnant, the support and interest of family members and of their former carers may be a precious practical and symbolic form of support. They may offer useful advice, encouragement and practical support around hospital visits and the like.

Spare-time activities as a source of support for young people in care

A young woman growing up in foster care was helped to keep up her interest in learning the flute by her foster carers, her school and her social worker over ten years. As she became a better musician, she needed more expensive instruments but the adults involved ensured that she secured them. Today, this young woman is a university graduate and working as a qualified music teacher . . .

For another less academically able or motivated young woman, participation in her beloved school choir served as an important incentive for her to remain in school beyond school leaving age. The choir may not have helped her achieve better results but delaying exit from school may have assisted her to develop important social skills and assets.

(Taken from Gilligan, 2007, p. 97, quoted in Bond, 2008, p. 53)

As young people enter the world in adult roles as worker or parent, volunteer or faith community member and so on, it may be a very important part of the role of current or former carers, or a significant adult or adults who have offered a nurturing role to the young person, to offer various forms of background support, occasional respite accommodation, a weekly meal, help with washing clothes, or encouragement when new ventures start to unravel as in a new course or applying for a new job. This kind of coaxing, coaching and cajoling is part and parcel of what every parent does and what every young person needs. Every young care-leaver especially needs it since they may have suffered so many blows to their confidence and self-belief along the way, and may have fewer ways of getting such help and encouragement when compared to young people growing up in their own home.

Some young people leaving care may have to relay on professionals to supply some of this help. But overall it seems much more desirable if it comes from people who realistically may be more likely to be part of their future network over the long haul – members of their birth or carers' family network, of community or work-based networks and so on.

Possible gender differences in accessing support

In terms of ability to access or use support, there is some evidence that there may be differences between boys and girls in how well they do this. Research on care leavers by Marsh and Peel (1999) is relevant here. Their work suggests that the social networks of young people leaving residential care may be smaller than the networks of those leaving foster care. Youngsters leaving residential care may thus have fewer people on whom potentially to draw for help when needed. In addition, Marsh and Peel suggest that young women leaving care may have stronger connections to mature women than boys have to mature men, when judged by the people they nominate as "family" (broadly understood). Relevant also to this point is the work of sociologist Sara Arber (2004), which studies how older adults access social support. She has found a tendency for women to be better at accessing social/emotional support from informal sources (for example, chatting to family, friends, neighbours), whereas men seem to rely on accessing social support through organised channels (for example, clubs, services, etc.). The implication of this various evidence may be that boys leaving residential care may be likely to be more isolated, whereas girls leaving foster care may be less likely to be isolated. These are suggested tendencies, not absolute certainties, in every instance. And making this point is certainly not meant to imply that girls leaving foster care may not need help. The point is that each young care-leaver's profile is based on a mix of history, care experiences, gender and so on. What we offer each young person needs to be well attuned to their profile and circumstances. How we offer help should also be respectful of their own capacity and agency, their views and preferences, their cultural background, and the assets and resources they have, including any continuing access to carers and birth family members.

Another big issue as young people reach care-leaving age is the issue of re-connecting with various family members. Contact may have withered or may have broken down acrimoniously. The passage of time may have airbrushed painful details from the picture and suppressed more difficult memories. The sense of a new beginning for the young care-leaver may inspire an understandable optimism about starting afresh with family ties. Sometimes, this optimism may prove well founded and things may work out well. But in other cases, the picture may be more complex. Initially, things may go well, but may then gradually unravel as old tensions and aggravations reassert themselves. Nevertheless, this process may offer a useful reality check and helpful clarification. It may also help the young person gauge the appropriate nature of contact in the future.

In all of these explorations, it may be invaluable for the young person to have a trusted adult in whom to confide and whom to consult. But given the very personal exposure involved in discussing such material, some young people may prefer to struggle on unaided, opting instead to process such material as best they can privately. Where this is the case, it may still be very valuable for a concerned adult who is well placed to stress to the young person that they are ready to listen if the need arises and that they also fully understand the very private nature of the project the young person has to take on.

> I think Mrs Barnett should win this award as she is one of a kind. She is always there and listens to me when I need her. She gives me good advice that helps with the problems I have. Mrs Barnett has a heart of gold. She isn't just there for me but for my friends too. She is the only person who believed in me since Year 7 when I first started high school. She never makes me feel lonely or insecure. She makes me feel special and warm inside. When I first started high school, I didn't have many friends but Mrs Barnett was there for me. She made me feel wanted and loved, which I never got at home.
>
> (Alana, 15, nominating her teacher, who became one of the 20 winners of the Believe in Me Awards 2007, organised by the Who Cares? Trust, quoted in Bond, 2008, p. 23)

The world of work

In a work-dominated economy and society, it is clear that social inclusion depends heavily on a place in the workforce. The sociability associated with life in the workplace may help to broaden a young person's social network (Bidart and Lavenu, 2005)

For the young person leaving care, finding a place in the world of work may also help to counteract the well-known risks of poverty, social isolation and boredom. Work can provide money, meaning and structure, social relationships, discipline and daily routine in a life that may otherwise be devoid of much of these. Work may also offer mentoring from a line manager who grows fond of the young person and recognises their needs. A concerned employer may offer motivation and opportunities for young people to re-enter training and education. Work may also offer friendships and activities for leisure; it may lead to companions with whom to share accommodation and holidays.

The world of work is not without its potential hazards for the young person. There may be a risk of exploitation, excessive hours, poor pay, harassment, bullying, health and safety hazards. Excessive hours at work may have an adverse effect on the academic performance and motivation of a young person still at school. But in our proper concern to protect the young person, we should be careful not to deprive him or her of opportunities for experiencing and coping with the real world. In a sense, the only way to become immune to the pressures of everyday living is to build up tolerance through controlled exposure. Engagement with the world of work combined with the support of a concerned adult may offer the right degree of controlled (and supported) exposure in an important arena of daily living. Work also offers money and a precious degree of associated freedom and initiative for the young person. This slight taster of autonomy may have additional significance for a youngster in care. US research suggests that early work experience may improve the employment opportunities of 'minority and economically disadvantaged urban youth later on' (Entwistle *et al*, 2000, p. 294).

Young people in care may lack some of the confidence and connections that can help many youngsters to get their first start in the world of work. Helping young people in care make the transition to the workforce should rely on supporting them to find mainstream opportunities rather than setting up specialist schemes for them alone (or for them and other vulnerable youngsters) that risk further ghettoising them and aggravating their sense of social stigma and exclusion. Carers and social workers can do a number of things that can be helpful – the kind of things which any concerned parent or relative might think of in the same circumstances.

What can carers do to assist the young person to find opportunities in the world of work?

- They can check out possible contacts in their own network of relatives, friends, neighbours and work colleagues for possible leads about vacancies.

- They can consult local employers for suggestions about the best strategy for securing work or work experience for the young person.

- They can help the young person to identify and value short-term or part-time options, which may be a valuable first step in gaining confidence and contacts.

- They can support the young person actively in pursuing any opportunities for school-organised work experience that may emerge.

- They can help the young person to think about contacts they may have in the neighbourhood or in families of friends or relatives who may make suggestions as to possible full-time or part-time work opportunities to pursue, and crucially also how to do so.

- They can explore with the young person how a hobby or interest may open up employment opportunities.

- They can help introduce the young person to other young people close in age and, ideally, in social or cultural background, who may have successfully made the break into the world of work. Such role models may be a valuable source of inspiration, encouragement and information.

- They can consult the school for suggestions they may have.

- They can help the young person to prepare a competent but realistic curriculum vitae (CV), in particular, by helping the young person to note experience, interests, skills, and talents which they may otherwise overlook.

- They can help a young person to polish their telephone presentation skills.

- They can help the young person to prepare for and rehearse interviews, possibly by getting a local employer to do a mock interview.

- They can encourage the young person to take up voluntary opportunities which may lead on to paid opportunities (e.g. voluntary work in an old people's home may open up possibility of locum shifts as a care assistant for a candidate showing promise).

- They can encourage the young person to check out mainstream training schemes.

- They can make a case to social services to subsidise an employer up to 100 per cent if necessary to take on a young person for a specified period (to give vital experience and the possibility of an invaluable employer's reference).

- They can help the young person to make the necessary preparations to ensure a professional image in front of the employer (presentable appearance and dress, personal organisation to ensure enhanced punctuality, general attitude and demeanour).

Part-time work: Examples of possible job options for young people in care

Babysitter
Fast food outlet serving assistant
Hairdresser
Kitchen assistant in hotels, guesthouses or public houses
Paper round
Petrol station attendant
Shop assistant
Supermarket check out assistant
Volunteer worker
Waiter/waitress

- They may help a young person with the talent, ideas and drive to set up their own micro-business, as in the case of the young girl who lived with Kate Cairns and her family, who had a small business rearing ducks, partly due to her deep love and knowledge of these feathered friends (Cairns, 2002).

What can social workers do?

The following are relevant points adapted from those listed in Gilligan (2008). Social workers can help young people to derive maximum gain from participation in recreational and part-time work experiences by:

- giving due attention, in key decisions and planning, to the potential benefits of recreational and work-related experiences in the lives of young people in care;

- helping to encourage and nurture such interests in young people in care;

- providing training and support to carers in this regard;

- ensuring briefing of new carers to maximise chances of their preserving connections to existing recreational interests for the young person, when he or she moves between care settings (Fong et al, 2006);

- appreciating how gender may lead to different experiences and opportunities for support and resilience for boys and girls in care;

- appreciating the power of positive role models for young people in care, for example, the specific (and often under-recognised) contribution that male foster carers may be able to make (Denuwalaere and Bracke, 2007, Gilligan, 2000c);

- recognising the value of continuity in care placements and relationships into young adulthood beyond the "official" care leaving age (Cashmore and Paxman, 2006; Courtney and Dworsky, 2006; Wade and Dixon, 2006) and the need to avoid premature rupturing of viable placements at what may be both a psychologically vulnerable developmental stage and, effectively, an arbitrary administrative cut-off point in a young person's care career.

Approaching potential employers

While fast food joints, service stations, supermarkets, other retail chains, and the armed forces may seem the more obvious options for young job seekers who are in or leaving care, it is important not to forget some less obvious possibilities: for example, hotels, restaurants, farms, social service organisations, hospitals, sporting organisations, law practices, media companies, voluntary bodies, airports, shipping and other transport services.

Below are some examples of young people's various pathways into the world of work.

> The key to horse dealing is to say one thing and let them give you another. I sold me last horse there for £800 but what I was really looking for was seven so I asked for £850 and then he bargained me down to eight. I always come out on top. I always come out with a good profit 'cos I'm real determined when I'm selling, d'ye know that type of way? You get an awful lot of fellas coming up, 'Ah, she's a girl, she doesn't know what she's talking about. Here, I'll give you this and I'll give you that.' But you've to play it tough and act real cool. 'Ah, you go on about your business. If you don't want this horse then don't buy it. What I'm looking for is what I'm looking for.' Then you come out on top and they know who they're dealing with. I kind of learned from me da – the tricks of the trade . . .
>
> *(Sonya Dunne, a teenager reflecting on the art of horse-dealing, in Ogden, 1999)*

I started working as a child when I was about 11 and full time when I was 16. I worked for a newsagent, filling up shelves and helping over the counter a couple of nights a week and on Saturdays. I've been a milk girl in my day, up at the crack of dawn delivering milk, and I've also worked in a café. Some of the money I managed to keep, especially in the café because of the tips that my father didn't know about. But most of it, I never saw it again after that. But it gave me some independence, some sense that I could do something for myself and maybe one day get out.

(Adult respondent in research study of the link between childhood abuse and neglect and adult depression who, on the basis of this and later positive work experiences, ultimately proved resilient in the face of adversity, quoted in Bifulco and Moran, 1998, p.165)

A boy who acquired an interest in tropical fish from his foster father gained a summer job in a local pet shop over two summer holidays based on his new expertise.

(Drawn from example in Gilligan, 2000a, p.118)

POINTS TO CONSIDER

How can concerned adults offer the right kind of support to young people to find work? Think of young people you know in your family circle or in your professional network. Have they found a way into the world of work? What helped them to do so? What have been the good or bad points of their experience? What lessons can you learn for your work with young people?

How can we help young people to keep links with carers and other concerned adults? How can we help young people to see that to go back into education remains open for them should they wish to use it? Do you know a young person who has done this? If so, what lessons can you learn from their experience?

9 Conclusion

© John Birdsall Photography

After growing up moving from family to family, school to school and social worker to social worker, the most exciting thing for me was the thought of getting my own tenancy - having my own place for the first time. And if it wasn't for the support from the nice people around me and many second chances, I would not have managed with the money and the forms and the cooking type of stuff. It's taken me nearly four years of living alone to get things right.

(Young person, quoted in Bond, 2008, p. 102)

Conclusion

There is an upbeat message in this book. Children can do well in difficult circumstances and, given favourable opportunities, children in the care system or other vulnerable children may do better than expected. In helping vulnerable young people to do well in care, it is often the detail of what is done that matters. If we want to know how to help a young person, it is important that we seek to understand carefully their particular history and their experience, to learn about their social networks, to learn about their interests and preferences. We need to know the specific meaning of the relationships, events and losses in their life. If we know the people and things that are important to the young person - and why - then there is a better chance that we can connect with this youngster in a way that will make a positive difference.

This book is part of an emerging school of thinking in "helping" services which sees helping as a partnership between people in need, people in their social networks and professional systems. In this approach, helping seeks to identify and build on the existing strengths and capacities within the person and their social context. The emphasis is on what the person can do, what the person is good at, what support lies waiting to be tapped, what is possible. Helping is about cultivating the "agency" of the young person, about seeing them as active agents in their own development. Problems and vulnerabilities are not to be ignored or discounted, but neither are they to be allowed to dominate. "One size fits all" solutions are generally to be avoided, since each person is unique and needs his or her own specific package of help.

It is essential to remember that a series of players can make a difference to the progress of a young person in care. Clearly the carer/parent is important. Their commitment, support and guidance can be key influences. Social workers can play a key role in offering the right degree of support to carers and young people and other people with a positive contribution to make. Members of the child's family of origin and other people close to the child can also play a valuable part. Social service agencies can offer support, encouragement and resources to the other relevant players. They can remove roadblocks to helping and they can give positive messages about what is useful and helpful to do.

It is also important how adults think about the child. The child is not a passive bystander in his or her own development and progress, but an active agent, and must be treated as an essential partner in planning and working for his or her own progress. This does not mean that young people are put on a pedestal with the adult carers and professionals merely executing their wishes and commands. But it is to say that the young people have unique insights into their own needs and experiences, and they have *agency* in terms of helping to influence their own progress and destiny. If these are ignored, then any intervention is likely to be all the poorer and less relevant for that.

Help can come in many forms but always through *relationships*. It does not come only through formal services or professional channels. The care and concern of carers and family members are likely to be very important. Sometimes, also, chance connections children make with interested adults in their family, community or school networks may prove very influential in helping a child move forward. There is often hidden capacity for healing within the child and the social networks surrounding the child which lies waiting to be tapped and released. The professional task is to recognise the potential for such healing and give it space to emerge.

Where there may be many problems in the young person's life, it is not necessary to solve them all at once. Getting progress in even one area may develop forward momentum. It may give the child and the adults around him or her the message that change is possible and that things can get better. Children in care, for example, may often become trapped in a negative downward spiral of ever-increasing difficulties. They may also be victims of a barely concealed pessimism among adults that nothing in the situation can improve or make a difference. Even small steps forward can be an important challenge to such negative thinking. To put a brake on a spiral of declining hope and to begin to turn the spiral in an upward positive direction can do untold good for self-esteem and morale. Suddenly things begin to look different to the child and to the adults around him or her. We should also remember that the seeds of what we do today may only bear fruit much later, a point emphasised by Sacker and Schoon (2007) in relation to influencing attitudes to a possible return to education at a later point for those who may have 'missed the boat during their teens or early twenties'. Young people who have had rocky experiences may need to be given more time before they can steady their boat. All is not lost if things are not going perfectly by 20 years of age. There is still time.

It is also important not to sacrifice the detail of good care on the altar of long-term plans which may take some time to come to fruition or which may prove frail in implementation. Longer-term planning is clearly important but not at the expense of careful attention to the detail of the child's needs today. Helping begins with doing something useful today, or more likely facilitating key adults to do something useful right now.

Without exception, vulnerable children do well because of the interest and commitment of at least one concerned adult. The adult's relationship with the child may be the crucial factor in the child's progress in releasing the child's potential.

> I moved to Sue and Tony's six days before Christmas, when I was nearly 16. They barely knew me but welcomed me into their home and gave me a fabulous Christmas . . . By January, I knew I wanted to stay and they knew they wanted to look after me. The problem was that they were only respite carers and, as I was 16, I was encouraged to leave and go into supported lodgings. But they fought for me, went to panel and became my carers.
>
> When most people had given up on me, they saw a young person who needed love, guidance and support. They gave me all of these things – helping me to get 11 GCSEs and then A Levels against all the odds.
>
> *(Sophy, 21, nominating her foster carers for the Believe in Me Awards 2007, organised by the Who Cares? Trust, quoted in Bond, 2008, pp. 44-5)*

DO'S AND DON'TS OF RESILIENCE-LED PRACTICE

- **Value stability in placement arrangements**

  Be slow to disrupt a placement which is a viable going concern, purely because it belongs to the wrong administrative category.

- **Value continuity in meaningful relationships**

  Value relationships that the child values.

- **Be patient**

  Appreciate that many young people in care may get there in the end in terms of being reasonably mature and competent adults, but it may take them longer because of all that has happened to them in their young lives.

- **Allow for some wobbles along the way**

  For many young people leaving care, the first few years may prove quite a rocky patch. Indeed, it may not be until the mid-twenties and beyond that things begin to settle down. So do not give up hope if things seem not to be going right in the first few years.

- **Value the young person being able to remain with their carer beyond the official care leaving age**

  Support carers and young people who wish for this to happen and make this scenario a more "normal" part of provision.

- **Value the child making sense of what has happened in the past**

  Help the child to understand what has happened, and do this at his or her pace.

- **Value positive school experience**

  Value educational and social attainment at school.

- **Value hobbies, interests and talents**

  Value what interests and rewards the child.

- **Value friendships, especially with children outside care**

  Help to keep friendships alive.

- **Value a child's connections to concerned adults**

  Help the child to tap into the concern and interest of adults in their natural social network.

- **Value appropriate opportunities for the child to take decisions and responsibility**

  Be alert to such opportunities in the different arenas in which the child lives out his or her life.

- **Avoid stereotypes of young people in care**

  Remember, each child is different – they may share some surface characteristics but each has his or her own unique history.

- **Avoid oversimplified "solutions" to the needs of young people in care**

  Remember "one size fits all" approaches don't work in a field as complex as working with children in care.

Bibliography

Ajayi, S. and Quigley, M., (2006) 'By degrees: care leavers in higher education' Ch. 5, in E. Chase, A. Simon and S. Jackson (eds) *In Care and After: A positive response*, London: Routledge

Andersson, G. (1999) 'Children in residential and foster care: a Swedish example', *International Journal of Social Welfare*, 8:4, pp.253-266

Andreou, C. (2000) 'Adolescents in care: the sense of homelessness', *Journal of Child Psychotherapy*, 26:1, pp.69-78

Arber, S. (2004) 'Gender, marital status and ageing: linking material, health, and social resources', *Journal of Aging Studies,* 18, pp.91-108

Argent, H. (ed) (1995) *See You Soon: Contact with children looked after by local authorities*, London: BAAF

Argent, H. (1998) *Whatever Happened to Adam? Stories of disabled people who were adopted or fostered*, London: BAAF

Argent, H. and Kerrane, A. (1997) *Taking Extra Care: Respite, shared and permanent care for children with disabilities*, London: BAAF

Baldry, S. and Kemmis, J. (1998) 'The quality of child care in one local authority: a user study', *Adoption & Fostering*, 22:3, pp.34-41

Barker, G. (1998) 'Non-violent males in violent settings: an exploratory qualitative study of prosocial low-income adolescent males in two Chicago (USA) neighbourhoods', *Childhood*, 5:4, pp.437-461

Barn, R. (ed.) (1999) *Working with Black Children and Adolescents in Need*, London: BAAF

Berridge, D. (1985) *Children's Homes*, Oxford: Basil Blackwell

Bidart, C. and Lavenu, D. (2005) 'Evolution of personal networks and life events', *Social Networks:* 27:4, pp.359-376

Biehal, N. (1999) 'Partnership and leaving care' in J. Masson, C. Harrison and A. Pavlocvic (eds.) *Lost and Found: Making and remaking working partnerships with parents of children in the care system*, Aldershot: Arena

Bifulco, A. and Moran, P. (1998) *Wednesday's Child: Research into women's experience of neglect and abuse in childhood, and adult depression*, London: Routledge

Bolger, K., Patterson, C. and Kupersmidt, J. (1998) 'Peer relationships and self-esteem among children who have been maltreated', *Child Development*, 69:4, pp.1171-1197

Bond, H. (ed) (2005) *'If you don't stick with me, who will?' The challenges and rewards of foster care*, London: BAAF

Bond, H. (2008) *Ten Top Tips for Preparing Care Leavers*, London: BAAF

Borge, A. (1996) 'Developmental pathways of behaviour problems in the young child: factors associated with continuity and change', *Scandinavian Journal of Psychology*, 37, pp.195–220

Bowlby, J. (1988) *A Secure Base: Clinical applications of attachment theory*, London: Routledge

Brennan, E. (2007) 'I was raised by the nuns', *The Guardian Weekend*, 17 February, p.14 *www.guardian.co.uk/weekend/story/0,,2013086,00.html*

Brooks, F. and Magnusson, J. (2007) 'Physical activity as leisure: the meaning of physical activity for the health and well-being of adolescent women', *Health Care for Women International*, 28, pp.69-87

Buchanan, A. (1997) 'The Dolphin Project: the impact of the Children Act', Ch. 7, in C. Cloke and M. Davies (eds.) *Participation and Empowerment in Child Protection*, Chichester: Wiley

Bullock, R., Little, M. and Millham, S. (1993) *Going Home: The return of children separated from their family*, Aldershot: Dartmouth

Cairns K. (2002) *Attachment, Trauma and Resilience*, London: BAAF

Cashmore, J., and Paxman, M. (1996) *Longitudinal Study of Wards Leaving Care*, Sydney: NSW Dept. of Community Services

Cashmore, J. and Paxman, M.(2006) 'Predicting after-care outcomes: the importance of "felt security"', *Child and Family Social Work*, 11, pp.232–241

Chase, E., Knight, A. and Statham, J. (2008) *The Emotional Well-Being of Young People Seeking Asylum in the UK*, London: BAAF

Clarke, M. (1998) *Lives in Care: Issues for policy and practice in children's homes*, Dublin: Mercy Congregation and The Children's Research Centre, Trinity College, Dublin

Cooper, G. (1999) 'Unless of course, that horse is a therapist: ride for pride helps juvenile offenders stay on the right trail', *Networker*, March–April, pp.11–12 and 14

Cooper, A. and Webb, L. (1999) 'Out of the maze: permanency planning in a post-modern world', *Journal of Social Work Practice*, 13:2, pp.119–134

Courtney, M. and Dworsky, A. (2006) 'Early outcomes for young adults transitioning from out-of-home care in the USA', *Child and Family Social Work*, 11, pp.209–219

Daly, F and Gilligan, R. (2005) *Lives in Foster Care*, Dublin: Children's Research Centre, Trinity College Dublin

Daniel, B, Wassell, S. and Gilligan, R. (1999a) *Child Development for Child Care and Protection Workers*, London: Jessica Kingsley Publishers

Daniel, B., Wassell, S. and Gilligan, R. (1999b) ' "It's just common sense isn't it?": exploring ways of putting the theory of resilience into action', *Adoption & Fostering*, 23:3, pp.6–15

Denuwelaere, M. and Bracke, P. (2007) 'Support and conflict in the foster family and children's well-being: a comparison between foster and birth children', *Family Relations,* 56, pp.67-79

Department of Health (1999) *Mapping Quality in Children's Services: An evaluation of local responses to the Quality Protects Programme - National Overview Report,* London: Department of Health

Dickson, Z. (1995) 'A care leaver's perspective of care and contact', pp.152-162, in H. Argent (ed.) *See You Soon: Contact with children looked after by local authorities,* London: BAAF

Emond, R. (2002) 'Understanding the resident group', *Scottish Journal of Residential Child Care,* 1, pp. 30-40

Emond, R. (2002a); *Learning from their Lessons: A study of young people in residential care and their experiences of education,* Dublin: Children's Research Centre, Trinity College Dublin

Emond, R. (2002) 'Understanding the resident group', *Scottish Journal of Residential Child Care,* 1, pp. 30-40

Entwistle, D., Alexander, K. and Olson, S. L. (2000) 'Early work histories of urban youth', *American Sociological Review,* 65, pp.279-297

Fernandez, E. (2007) 'How children experience fostering outcomes: participatory research with children', *Child and Family Social Work,* 12, pp.349-359

Fletcher, B. (1993) *Not Just a Name: The views of young people in foster and residential care,* London: National Consumer Council

Fong, R., Schwab, J., and Armour M. (2006) 'Continuity of activities and child well-being for foster care youth', *Children and Youth Services Review,* 28, 11, pp.1359-1374

Francis, J. (2000) 'Investing in children's futures: enhancing the educational arrangements of "looked after" children and young people', *Child and Family Social Work,* 5:1, pp.23-33

Fraser, M., Richman, J. and Galinsky, M. (1999) 'Risk, protection and resilience: toward a conceptual framework for social work practice', *Social Work Research,* 23:3, pp.131-143

Freeman, I., Morrison, A., Lockhart, F. and Swanson, M. (1996) 'Consulting service users: the views of young people' in M. Hill and J. Aldgate (eds.) *Child Welfare Services: Developments in law, policy, practice and research,* London: Jessica Kingsley Publishers

Geenen, S. & Powers, L.E. (2007) 'Tomorrow is another problem: The experiences of youth in foster care during their transition into adulthood', *Children and Youth Services Review,* 29, pp. 1085-1101

Gilligan, R. (1999) 'Enhancing the resilience of children and young people in public care by mentoring their talents and interests', *Child and Family Social Work,* 4:3, pp.187-196

Gilligan, R. (2000a) 'Promoting resilience in children in foster care', Ch. 5, pp.107-126, in G. Kelly and R. Gilligan (eds.) *Issues in Foster Care: Policy, practice and research*, London: Jessica Kingsley Publishers

Gilligan, R. (2000b) 'Adversity, resilience and young people: the protective value of positive school and spare time experiences', *Children and Society*, 14:1, pp.37-47

Gilligan, R. (2000c) 'Men as foster carers – a neglected resource?', *Adoption & Fostering*, 24:2, pp.63-9

Gilligan, R. (2000d) 'The key role of social workers in promoting the well-being of children in state care: a neglected dimension of reforming policies', *Children and Society*, 14:4, pp.267-276

Gilligan R. (2007) 'Spare time activities for young people in care: what can they contribute to educational progress?' *Adoption & Fostering*, 31:1, pp. 92-99

Gilligan, R. (2008), 'Promoting resilience in young people in long term care: the relevance of roles and relationships in the domains of recreation and work', *Journal of Social Work Practice*, 22: 1, pp.37-50

Greeson, J. and Bowen, N. (2008) ' "She holds my hand" – the experiences of foster youth with their natural mentors', *Children and Youth Services Review*, 30, pp.1178-1188

Happer, H., McCreadie, J., and Aldgate, J. (2006) *Celebrating Success: What helps looked after children succeed*, Edinburgh: Social Work Inspection Agency

Harker, R., Dobel-Ober, D., Lawrence, J., Berridge, D., and Sinclair, R. (2003) 'Who takes care of education? Looked after children's perceptions of support for educational progress', *Child and Family Social Work*, 8: 2, pp.89-100.

Harris P. (ed) (2006) *In Search of Belonging: Reflections by transracially adopted people*, London: BAAF

Hartman, A. (1995) 'Diagrammatic assessment of family relationship', *Families in Society: The journal of contemporary human services*, 76:3, pp.111-122

Hartup, W. (1996) 'The company they keep: friendships and their developmental significance', *Child Development*, 67, pp.1-13

Hazel, N. (1981) *A Bridge to Independence*, Oxford: Basil Blackwell

Hill, M. (1999) 'What's the problem? Who can help? The perspectives of children and young people on their well-being and on helping professionals', *Journal of Social Work Practice*, 13:2, pp.135-145

Hindle, D. (1998) 'Growing up with a parent who has a chronic mental illness: one child's perspective', *Child and Family Social Work*, 3:4, pp.259-266

Hines, A., Merdinger, J. and Wyatt, P. (2005) 'Former foster youth attending college: resilience and the transition to young adulthood', *American Journal of Orthopsychiatry*, 75: 3, pp.381-394

Howe, D., Brandon, M., Hinings, D. and Schofield, G. (1999) *Attachment Theory, Child Maltreatment and Family Support*, London: Macmillan

Ince, L. (1998) *Making it Alone: A study of the care experiences of young black people*, London: BAAF

Iso-Ahola, S. (1997) 'A psychological analysis of leisure and health', Ch. 9, pp.131–144, in J. Haworth (ed.) *Work, Leisure and Well-Being*, London: Routledge

Jackson, S. and Martin, P. (1998) 'Surviving the care system: education and resilience', *Journal of Adolescence*, 21, pp.569-583

Jackson, S. and Thomas, N. (1999) *On the move again? What works in creating stability for looked after children*, Ilford: Barnardo's

Jardine, S. (1999) 'Transracial placements: an adoptee's perspective', Ch. 10, pp.147–156, in R. Barn (ed.) *Working with Black Children and Adolescents in Need*, London: BAAF

Jenkins, J. and Smith, M. (1990) 'Factors protecting children in disharmonious homes: maternal reports', *Journal of the American Academy of Child and Adolescent Psychiatry*, 29:1, pp.60-69

Johnson, B. (2008) 'Teacher-student relationships which promote resilience at school: a micro-level analysis of students' views', *British Journal of Guidance & Counselling*, 36, pp.385-398

Kahan, B. (1979) *Growing up in Care: Ten people talking*, Oxford: Blackwell

Laub, J. and Sampson, R. (2003) *Shared Beginnings, Divergent Lives: Delinquent boys to age 70*, Cambridge, Mass. : Harvard University Press

Lindsay, M. and Foley, T. (1999) 'Getting them back to school: touchstones of good practice in the residential care of young people', *Children and Society*, 13, pp.192–202

Luthar, S.S., Sawyer, J.A. & Brown, P.J. (2006) 'Conceptual issues in studies of resilience: Past, Present, and Future Research.' *Annals of the New York Academy of Sciences,* 1094, pp. 105-115

Mahoney, J. (2000) 'School extracurricular activity participation as a moderator in the development of antisocial patterns', *Child Development*, 71:2, pp.502–516

Mahoney, J. and Cairns, R. (1997) 'Do extra-curricular activities protect against early school drop out?' *Developmental Psychology*, 33, pp.241–253

Mahoney, J. and Stattin, H, (2000) 'Leisure activities and adolescent antisocial behavior: the role of structure and social context', *Journal of Adolescence*, 23, pp.113–127

Marsh, P and Peel, M (1999) *Leaving Care in Partnership: Family involvement with care leavers*, London: The Stationery Office

Martin, F. (1998) 'Tales of transition: self-narrative and direct scribing in exploring care-leaving', *Child and Family Social Work*, 3:1, pp.1–12

Martin, P. and Jackson, S. (2002) 'Educational success for children in public care: advice from high achievers', *Child and Family Social Work*, 7: 2, pp.121–130

Masten, A. and Coatsworth, J. (1998) 'The development of competence in favourable and unfavourable environments', *American Psychologist*, 53:2, pp.205–220

Maunders, D., Liddell, M., Liddell, M. and Green, S. (1999) *Young People Leaving Care and Protection*, Hobart: Australian Clearing House for Youth Studies

McAuley, C. and Trew, K. (2000) 'Children's adjustment over time in foster care: cross-informant agreement, stability and placement disruption', *British Journal of Social Work*, 30, pp.91–107

McTeigue, D. (1998) 'The use of focus groups in exploring children's experiences of life in care', pp.45–53, in D. Hogan and R. Gilligan (eds.) *Researching Children's Experience*, Dublin: Trinity College Children's Research Centre

National Foster Care Association (1993) *Making it Home*, London: National Foster Care Association

Noon, A. (2000) 'Improving mental health outcomes for looked after children', *Adoption & Fostering*, 24:2, p.83

Ogden, P. (1999) *Pony Kids*, London: Jonathan Cape Random House

Okitikpi, T. (1999) 'Educational needs of black children in care', Ch. 8, pp.107–127, in R. Barn (ed.) *Working with Black Children and Adolescents in Need*, London: BAAF

O'Neale, V. (2000) *Excellence Not Excuses: Inspection of services of ethnic minority children and families*, London: Department of Health

Page, R. and Clarke, G. (1977) *Who Cares? Young People in Care Speak Out*, London: National Children's Bureau

Posner, J. and Vandell, D. (1999) 'After-school activities and the development of low-income urban children: a longitudinal study', *Developmental Psychology*, 35:3, pp.868–879

Quinton, D., Rushton, A., Dance, D. and Mayes, D. (1997) 'Contact between children placed away from home and their birth parents: research issues and evidence', *Clinical Child Psychology and Psychiatry*, 2:3, pp.393–413

Quinton, D. and Rutter, M. (1988) *Parenting Breakdown: The making and breaking of inter-generational links*, Aldershot: Avebury

Rashid, S. (2000) 'The strengths of black families: appropriate placements for all', *Adoption & Fostering*, 24:1, pp.15–22

Romans, S., Martin, J., Anderson, J., O'Shea, M. and Mullen, P. (1995) 'Factors that mediate between child sexual abuse and adult psychological outcome', *Psychological Medicine*, 25, pp.127–142

Rönkä, A., Oravala, S. and Pulkkinen, L. (2002) ' "I met this wife of mine and things got onto a better track": turning points in risk development', *Journal of Adolescence*, 25, pp.47–63

Rowe, J., Cain, H., Hundleby, M. and Keane, A. (1984) *Long-Term Foster Care*, London: Batsford Academic

Rutter, M. (1990) 'Psychosocial resilience and protective mechanisms', Ch. 9, pp.181–214, in J. Rolf, A. Masten, D. Cicchetti and K. Nüchterlein, *Risk and Protective Factors in the Development of Psychopathology*, Cambridge: Cambridge University Press

Rutter, M. (1999) 'Resilience concepts and findings: implications for family therapy', *Journal of Family Therapy*, 21, pp.119–144

Ryan, T. and Walker, R. (2007) *Life Story Work* (3rd edn.), London: BAAF

Sacker, A. and Schoon, I. (2007) 'Educational resilience in later life: resources and assets in adolescence and return to education after leaving school at age 16', *Social Science Research*, 36, pp.873–896

Saleebey, D. (ed.) (1997) *The Strengths Perspective in Social Work* (2nd edn.), New York: Longman

Schofield, G. (1998) 'Making sense of the ascertainable wishes and feelings of insecurely attached children', *Child and Family Law Quarterly*, 10:4, pp.363–375

Schofield, G. (2003) *Part of the Family: Pathways through foster care*, London: BAAF

Schofield, G. and Brown, K. (1999) 'Being there: a family centre worker's role as a secure base for adolescent girls in crisis', *Child and Family Social Work*, 4:1, pp.21–31

Schofield G., Beek M. and Sargent K. (2000) *Growing up in Foster Care*, London: BAAF

Shah S. and Argent H. (2006) *Life Story Work: What it is and what it means*, London: BAAF

Sinclair, R. (1998) *The Education of Children in Need*, Dartington: Research in Practice

Sinclair, I. and Gibbs, I. (1998) *Children's Homes – A study in diversity*, Chichester: Wiley

Skinner, A. (1992) *Another Kind of Home: A review of residential child care*, Edinburgh: HMSO

Smith, C. and Carlson, B. (1997) 'Stress, coping and resilience in children and youth', *Social Service Review*, 71, pp.231–256

Stadler, C. (2007) '"Don't we deserve a decent education?"' *Adoption and Fostering*, 31:1, pp.11–12

Stein, M., Rees, G. and Frost, N. (1994) *Running the Risk: Young people on the streets of Britain today*, London: The Children's Society

Sturge-Moore L. (ed) (2005) *Could you be my Parent? Adoption and fostering stories*, London: BAAF

Sumpton, A. (1999) 'Communicating with and assessing black children', Ch. 6, pp.81–97, in R. Barn (ed.) *Working with Black Children and Adolescents in Need*, London: BAAF

Thiede Call, K. (1996) 'Adolescent work as an "arena of comfort" under conditions of family discomfort' in J. Mortimer and M. Finch (eds.) *Adolescents, Work, and Family: An intergenerational developmental analysis*, Thousand Oaks: Sage

Thoburn, J., Norford, L. and Rashid, S. (1998) *Permanent Family Placement for Children of Minority Ethnic Origin*, Norwich: University of East Anglia/ Department of Health

Thoits, P. (1983) 'Multiple identities and psychological well being: a reformulation and test of the social isolation hypothesis', *American Sociological Review*, 48, pp.174–187

Tracy, E. (1990) 'Identifying social support resources of at-risk families', *Social Work*, 35:3, pp.252–258

Trew, K. (1997) 'Time for sport? Activity diaries of young people', Ch. 7, pp.126–151, in J. Kremer, K. Trew and S. Ogle (eds.) *Young People's Involvement in Sport*, London: Routledge

Triseliotis, J., Borland, M. and Hill, M. (2000) *Delivering Foster Care*, London: BAAF

Triseliotis, J., Borland, M., Hill, M. and Lambert, L. (1995) *Teenagers and the Social Work Services*, London: HMSO

Unrau, Y.A., Seita, J.R. and Putney, K.S. (2008) 'Former foster youth remember multiple placement moves: a journey of loss and hope', *Children and Youth Services Review*, 30, pp.1256–1266

Wade, J. (2008) 'The ties that bind: support from birth families and substitute families for young people leaving care', *British Journal of Social Work*, 38, pp. 39–54

Wade, J. and Dixon, J. (2006) 'Housing and career outcomes for young people leaving care', *Child and Family Social Work*, 11, pp.199–208

Way, N. and Leadbetter, B. (1999) 'Pathways towards educational achievement among African American and Puerto Rican adolescent mothers: re-examining the role of social support from families', *Development and Psychopathology*, 11, pp.349–364

Werner, E. and Smith, R. (1992) *Overcoming the Odds: High risk children from birth to adulthood*, Ithaca: Cornell University

Yelloly, M. (1979) *Independent Evaluation of Twenty Five Placements*, Maidstone: Kent Family Placement Project

LIBRARY, UNIVERSITY OF CHESTER